Red Deer Management

A practical book for the management of
wild red deer in Scotland

Red Deer Commission   Inverness

Edinburgh   Her Majesty's Stationery Office

ISBN 0 11 491692 6

Contents

Acknowledgements

The Red Deer Commission wish to record their thanks to Dr Brian Mitchell and Mr I. A. Nicholson of the Institute of Terrestrial Ecology for their contributions to the text of this book and for their help and assistance throughout its production.

Similarly we wish to mark our appreciation to Mr D. J. Harrison, himself a member of the Commission, for his contribution on deer fencing and to the field and administrative staff of the Commission without whose services 'Red Deer Management' would never have been published.

We gratefully acknowledge the use of illustrations from:

Dr B. Mitchell, Plates 1, 2 and 3; Dr G. R. Miller, Plates 4, 5, 6, 7, 8, 9 and 11; Mr I. A. Nicholson, Plates 10, 14, 16, 17, 19 and 20; Mr I. S. Paterson, Plates 13, 15 and 18; Dr A. Watson, Plate 12.

The text was edited by Donald Omand, Department of Adult Education and Extra-Mural Studies, University of Aberdeen.

Innes Miller
Chairman
Red Deer Commission

Preface

While much has been written about the biology and management of red deer by scientists and others interested in the species, the Red Deer Commission have considered for some time that a practical up-to-date work of reference for stalkers, deer managers and deer forest owners ought to be compiled. The Commission hope that this modest publication helps to fill the gap.

It is generally believed that red deer originally came from Europe to Britain when the ice caps receded and, following the destruction of the natural forest, adapted from living in woodland to living on the hill.

The decline of the profitability of large-scale sheep farming introduced after the Highland Clearances, the advent of the Industrial Revolution and the popularity of the sport of stalking, resulted in a gradual increase in the deer population, until by 1977 there were 270,000 red deer in Scotland. On this scale deer are in territorial and grazing conflict with forestry and farming interests.

For many years deer were considered to be of little value other than for sport, but with the opening up of the European venison market in the early 1960s they began to be a significant source of income, and the revenue now obtainable from the sale of venison is an important economic consideration in the viability of estates.

In the interests of estates as well as the general economy of the Highlands it is important that deer management should be as efficient as possible and that any costs borne by agriculture and forestry on account of red deer should be reduced to a minimum.

The wildlife value of deer as a tourist attraction must not be under-rated, for as well as giving enjoyment they also provide employment in the hotel trade and in craft industries.

List of Plates

List of Figures

PART I   INTRODUCTION

Chapter 1   Red Deer: Habitat and Range

Most biologists now regard the red deer in Europe, and the closely related wapiti (elk) in Asia and North America, as all being racial forms of the one species, *Cervus elaphus*. Accepting this view, it is clear that red deer are successful and adaptable animals, being distributed, with some gaps, around the Temperate Zone of the Northern Hemisphere, between the latitudes of 30° and 65°. In Scotland they are towards the northern limit of their natural range.

Red deer have also been introduced successfully into various parts of the Southern Hemisphere, their most spectacular impact being in New Zealand where their progressive spread and increase in numbers over the past century have created special problems of habitat destruction and soil erosion.

Red deer from the Continent have been introduced into English deer-parks and Scottish deer-forests, ostensibly to prevent in-breeding or to improve size and, because of the flow of blood-stock between deer-parks and deer-forests within Britain, it is difficult to gauge the effect on local populations and to identify true native stock.

Visitors from abroad who may be familiar with red deer in their own countries, are generally surprised by the fact that Scottish red deer tend to be much smaller and occupy a different kind of habitat. These differences reflect the harsher conditions in which the animals have to live rather than differences in their genetic make-up, as deer of Scottish origin have proved capable of considerable growth when reared or released in more favourable habitats.

Throughout the world, red deer occupy a variety of habitats and different forms of terrain from low to high altitudes. Generally they live in close association with many kinds of woodlands: for example, relatively dry Mediterranean scrub, moist wooded marshes and river sides, natural deciduous and coniferous woodlands, and, of course, man-made plantations. They avoid the inner sections of thick forests and do not normally settle on plains unless there are patches of woodland. Red deer prefer open woodlands or woodland-edge situations.

It is not immediately obvious why red deer survive and even thrive on open hill-land in Scotland; here they live at appreciably higher population densities than almost anywhere else in the world, albeit with poorer growth and breeding performance. Certainly the progressive loss of the natural forests in Scotland has forced the deer to adapt to a changed habitat, but it is the success with which this adaptation has taken place that is in many ways so surprising.

To red deer, woodland seems important mainly as a place of security where they can hide. Hill-land may provide a similar sense of security where deer can detect any source of danger in good time to take the necessary action. 'To see or not be seen' may be a crucial factor in habitat selection. Woodlands are used for shelter, as well as cover, by deer.

Big herbivorous mammals, like red deer, tend to live in large groups on open land and in smaller groups in woodland, thereby achieving mutual protection, a lesser chance of detection, or a greater chance of escape.

In the movement of red deer between their summer and winter ranges, stags spend a much greater proportion of the year on low ground and tend to winter lower down than hinds. With hinds it is usually the poorer animals and those with calves which are first down in autumn and spend longest on low ground. With these the poorest yearling stags, ie the most hind-like knobbers are found. The better hinds, yearlings and calves tend to winter a little higher with appreciably more movement between night-time and day-time feeding areas—behavioural patterns which have important management implications.

PART II BIOLOGY OF THE RED DEER

Chapter 2 Reproduction

The Annual Cycle

Red deer have marked responses to the seasonal changes in their environment and their life history shows distinctive annual cycles.

Day-length is the main factor to which the annual cycle is geared. It changes smoothly and predictably over the year and many plants and animals have evolved special mechanisms which are sensitive to changes in day-length as the main ways of synchronising their life cycles with the seasons. Other factors (sex, age, breeding status, condition and nutrition) merely advance or retard to a small extent the basic patterns and responses. Day-length also controls the sexual cycles in stags and hinds, though in rather different ways.

The advantages of having a built-in calendar, and the means of maintaining it, are obvious. It is better for the hind to support a young calf during the summer, and to be pregnant over the winter, since lactation makes much bigger demands than pregnancy.

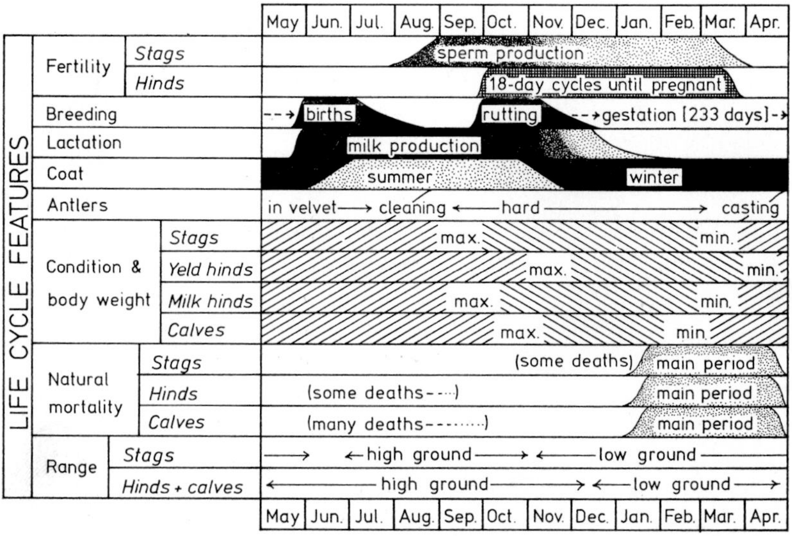

		May	Jun.	Jul.	Aug.	Sep.	Oct.	Nov.	Dec.	Jan.	Feb.	Mar.	Apr.
Fertility	*Stags*						sperm production						
	Hinds							18-day cycles until pregnant					
Breeding				- -→ births			rutting	- -→ gestation [233 days] -→					
Lactation				milk production									
Coat					summer				winter				
Antlers		in velvet → cleaning ←— hard ————→ casting											
Condition & body weight	*Stags*				max.						min.		
	Yeld hinds					max.					min.		
	Milk hinds					max.					min.		
	Calves					max.					min.		
Natural mortality	*Stags*						(some deaths)	main period					
	Hinds		(some deaths - - -)					main period					
	Calves		(many deaths - - - - - - -)					main period					
Range	*Stags*	—→ ←— high ground ——→ ←——— low ground ——											
	Hinds + calves	←——— high ground ————→ ←— low ground —→											
		May	Jun.	Jul.	Aug.	Sep.	Oct.	Nov.	Dec.	Jan.	Feb.	Mar.	Apr.

Figure 1 The main features of the annual life cycle of red deer on Scottish hill-land.

12

Aspects of the life-cycle, especially reproduction, growth, condition and natural mortality, have been studied intensively but much has still to be learned. The broad features of the annual cycle are summarised in Figure 1 where, for convenience, the 'deer year' extends from early May to late April.

The Stag

The age at which a stag becomes sexually mature depends to a large extent on its rate of growth, faster growth leading to earlier maturity. The actual period of the year when a stag is fertile depends on day-length, age and condition. Prime stags, therefore, became fertile appreciably earlier than the young, the old and those in poor condition.

Antler development is related to the sexual cycle. Stags produce sperm throughout the time that they have their annual hard antlers, roughly from August to March in a full-grown beast. In broad terms, a high level of male sex hormone leads to sperm production and the cessation of antler growth (ie loss of velvet and hardening of the antlers), whereas a low level of sex hormone leads to cessation of sperm production, antler casting, and antler regrowth. Thus, in an adult stag, the antlers grow when the sex hormone level is low, and when the stag is not fertile. Stags in very poor condition tend to cast their antlers later than the better stags, confirming that the condition of the animal affects its responses to the male sex hormone.

The Hind

In principle, much the same factors affect puberty, fertility, and the sexual cycle in hinds as in stags, although they may operate and interact in different ways. The effect of day-length was confirmed following the transportation of red deer to the Southern Hemisphere, where they bred exactly six months out of step with those in the Northern Hemisphere.

The earliest that puberty normally occurs in either sex is during their second autumn (as yearlings) but, under Scottish conditions, it is usually one or two years later in most hinds. Research has shown that sexual maturity in hinds depends mainly on body weight and it is unusual to find a hind that reaches puberty at less than around 95 lb (43 kg) larder carcase weight or an equivalent live weight of 146 lb (66 kg).

The fertility of an adult hind is also dependent on her body weight and it appears that there are critical levels in weight and condition below which the ability to ovulate is 'switched off'. However, hinds on the borderline between good and poor condition tend to ovulate late during the rutting season. In general, however, those in poor condition, by failing to ovulate, may avoid suffering the added burdens of pregnancy and lactation and have a year in which to recover weight and condition. Virtually every hind which ovulates becomes pregnant.

Some hinds seem better than others in the efficiency of breeding. Samples taken of milk hinds and their calves indicated that those with the biggest calves showed the highest body weights and fat reserves, and were also pregnant. Therefore, while some hinds breed a year and miss a year, there are undoubtedly others which tend to breed most years. In addition there are the 'poor doers' which breed infrequently.

The Rut

The times of the year during which stags and hinds are fertile differ in duration. Stags, being fertile for longer than hinds, are potentially capable of breeding throughout the time that their antlers are hard, ie roughly from late August until late March. Adult hinds prevented from being mated come into season about every 18 days from around mid to late September until late March.

The rut appears to start when the hinds come into season, but stags are slow to respond initially so that some of the first ovulations may be missed. Although studies in a number of parts of Scotland have shown that conceptions may be spread over total periods of about 100 days, the majority are concentrated into October. Therefore, the rut, like the calving season, shows a quick build-up, a sharp peak of activity and takes a longer time to tail off.

Stags and hinds in best condition and in the prime of life are the earliest to breed. Hinds reach their prime appreciably earlier in life than stags. With stags, the ability to hold hinds in the rut is strongly dependent on their body weight and condition; the smaller and younger males take possession of the hinds only when the bigger and older stags are spent. There is no evidence that hummel (ie unantlered) stags are more successful than antlered stags in rutting, nor are they, on average, larger than normal stags.

Pregnancy

Pregnancy lasts about 233 days (33 weeks), a week or so either way covering the extremes, with most calves born between late May and late June. Although certain areas are characterised by the births being earlier or later than average, a fortnight covers the maximum difference in average calving dates between different populations in Scotland. Similarly, there tend to be early years and late years, with two weeks appearing to cover the maximum variation in one population.

Birth Rate

Although red deer have four nipples, suggesting that multiple births occurred earlier in their evolution, they normally have one calf at a time. Twinning is rare. Available information indicates a rate of not more than one case in several hundred conceptions on Scottish hill-land, with a rather higher rate in woodlands. There is at least one case of triplet embryos recorded in German forests.

For animals like red deer that have an annual breeding period and a potential output of one calf per mature hind per year, the maximum calving rate can be calculated. It depends primarily on the age of puberty. Thus, in ideal circumstances, where hinds reach puberty as yearlings (calving first at 2 years) and breed every year thereafter, an annual birth rate of around 70 calves/100 hinds can be expected. The corresponding birth rates for hinds reaching puberty as 2 and 3 year olds would be 60/100 and 50/100 respectively. In practice these maximum rates are seldom attained (see Chapter 4), since at least some adult hinds 'go yeld' each year in most populations. The comparatively low birth rate on Scottish hill-land (40 to 45 calves/100 hinds) can be explained by the late attainment of puberty coupled with the poorer breeding success of adult hinds.

Calves

Calves grow rapidly from the time of their birth in June until mid-autumn, increasing by some five to six times in body weight. From then until late March there is a growth check when they tend to lose weight and condition. Growth begins again in late April. Curiously enough, skeletal growth continues, albeit slowly, over the winter months, the calves becoming bigger but thinner. Other classes of immature deer show similar patterns of change, although the rates of increase and decrease are much less than in calves over the winter months. Yearling stags on average seem to be poorer in condition than yearling hinds.

The fact that calves tend to achieve their maximum levels in weight and condition a little later than their mothers (Figure 1) simply shows that they are living at the expense of their mothers' reserves.

Lactation

Lactation can be lengthy in red deer hinds, making it difficult to decide when the majority on Scottish hill-land become completely dry. Some milk hinds, but not all, are dry by late December to mid-January. Pregnant milk hinds tend to dry up earlier than non-pregnant ones, some of which can continue to lactate into the next calving period. For example, a group of hinds which were shot for research purposes during early July were found to be producing milk although they showed no signs of recent pregnancy. There have been many reports of hinds, apparently without current calves, allowing yearlings to suckle, although, of course, many of those could have been milk hinds that had lost calves.

Studies on captive hinds have shown that their milk production increases steadily until about 70 days after giving birth, that is until September. A number were still producing milk, albeit very slowly, after 280 days. The quality of milk was found to increase over the first part of lactation, reaching a steady concentration thereafter. Tests showed that it had, on average, twice the energy content of cow's milk.

Chapter 3   **Digestion and Diet**

Digestive System

A characteristic feature of ruminants is the large size of the digestive tract. The whole 'gralloch' of a red deer comprises 24 to 36% of the weight of the whole animal.

The success and usefulness of red deer depend to a large extent on the fact that they belong to the ruminant group of mammals which are the most efficient at digesting forage and of which there are two main families, namely the horn-bearing *Bovidae* (cattle, sheep, goats and antelopes) and the antler-bearing *Cervidae* (deer). Of the two, cervids are much more restricted in range to the colder and moister parts of the world, and they are fewer in species. Although reindeer may be the oldest domesticated meat producers, most farmed livestock are bovids. It is important to know why ruminants are so successful in their distribution and abundance around the world and why they are so important to mankind as producers of meat.

Since forage is much more difficult to digest than flesh, those animals living on plant material, the herbivores, have larger and more complex digestive tracts than predators and scavengers. In general, the more complex the digestive system, the more efficient the process of digestion. Ruminants with their four-chambered stomachs represent an evolutionary peak in digestive efficiency.

The difficulties of extracting energy and nutrients from plant material arise from its tough cell walls—consisting largely of cellulose (energy-rich but indigestible)—and from relatively low concentrations of nutrients in the cell contents, especially in leaves and stems. Curiously enough, it is only a few species of invertebrates, and several kinds of microbes which produce their own chemical agents (enzymes) for digesting cellulose, and vertebrate herbivores enlist the help of a variety of micro-organisms nurtured within their digestive tract. The first stomach compartment, or rumen (ie the 'big bag') is really a large fermentation chamber where these microbes help to break down the forage. Having this special facility at the beginning of the digestive tract allows for food to be given a good soaking and to be partly digested before re-chewing and passing on for further digestion and absorption.

Rumination or chewing the cud is the conspicuous feature of ruminants, and they can subsist, when necessary, on the poorest quality of forage materials. Other herbivores exist either by restricting themselves to higher quality plant materials such as seeds, nuts and new growth, or by settling for a lower efficiency of digestion and a greater throughput, or by reingesting some of their own faecal pellets.

Feeding Behaviour

In ruminants, feeding is intermittent, with a number of active cycles of foraging followed by chewing the cud each day. It is not known for certain how many feeding cycles red deer have each day on hill-land or whether this varies individually or seasonally. Observation in one area of hill-land during winter showed that different groups of deer were all doing much the same at given times of the day, and it appeared that over 24 hours there were three distinct periods of active feeding with three slightly shorter periods of rumination. One complete feeding cycle appeared to last about 8 hours, but this could have been a feature of winter in that area; feeding cycles may be shorter when forage digestibility is higher. A long period of rumination around the middle of the day is usual on hill-land when, having reached the highest part of their daily range, the deer tend to rest up and chew the cud.

Diet

Listing the plant species that red deer eat shows simply that there are few types which the animals will not touch at some time of year. Some forms of plant material are more abundant in rumen samples than they are in the field, indicating that feeding is selective. Soft leaves are taken in preference to stems, and new growth (green material) to old growth or dead material. A good deal of research has been done, mainly on other species of deer, to find the chemical factors leading to the selection or avoidance of different kinds of plant material. In general, the preferred material is high in protein and low in fibre.

It is not known for certain why some tree species such as Norway spruce are browsed more than, say, Scots pine or why bark stripping is particularly severe on Lodgepole pine and not on Scots pine.

There are interesting patterns in the annual cycles of food selection by red deer in various habitats. Grasses, sedges and herbs are taken throughout the year, whereas browse is eaten mainly during winter and early spring. This kind of feeding pattern is related to the way in which grassy and woody vegetation change throughout the year; grass varies much more with more die-back, greater loss of protein and increase of fibre content during the non-growing season. Even so, given a choice, deer will select the softest green material. Dwarf-shrubs, principally heather, are invaluable as winter forage. Therefore, management aimed at the complete replacement of heather by grassland would be a mistake.

Because of the importance of ruminants as farm livestock, their food requirements are well understood. In tables published for livestock feeding, requirements are usually given separately for maintenance alone, growth and fattening, the late stages of pregnancy and lactation, each being related to body weight. Lactation tends to double the requirements of an animal to maintain its body weight.

Contrary to popular belief, it has been shown that red deer have about 30% higher requirements per unit of body weight than sheep, probably because of their higher level of activity. Several species of deer have been shown to eat more in summer and less in winter: banking excess energy as fat during the summer and autumn may have been evolved for living in an environment with distinct seasons of plenty and of privation.

As might be expected the food intake is large. As a rough guide, a typical population on Scottish hill-land would consume its own weight in fresh forage over 10 to 14 days.

The chewing of bones and cast antlers which occurs throughout the hill-range of red deer in Scotland is much rarer elsewhere, especially in woodland habitats where cast antlers may persist for years. Shortage of phosphorus (rather than calcium) appears to be the crucial factor on the upland soils of Scotland which are mostly low in this element.

Chapter 4 **Performance**

'Performance' covers those variable features of animals (eg reproduction, body growth and longevity) which affect their productivity and population turn-over. In broad terms, the production potential of a population is governed partly by the number of young born each year, and by the average annual weight gain of individuals in the population. What can be harvested from a population is limited, however, by the processes of natural wastage (ie natural mortality and senescence), and an important consideration is the extent to which these can be reduced or offset by management factors (see Part III). In assessing performance and its variability in red deer, we must consider how stags and hinds tend to change with age, and how they respond to changes or differences in environment. Environmental influences on performance comprise:

(i) 'habitat factors' including the physical ones affecting the 'energy cost of living' (eg temperature, wind and rain, and the presence of shelter), and the biological resources on which the animals depend (ie main kinds of vegetation present, and their amounts);

(ii) 'population density' and 'competition' (ie numbers of mouths competing for the same food);

(iii) parasites and diseases (see Chapter 5).

Up to now, research on the performance of red deer in Scotland has been concentrated mainly on hill-land populations, with rather less attention to the deer in woodland habitats. Nonetheless, some aspects of performance and its variability are shown here in graph form using information from one population at relatively high population density on Scottish hill-land and another at lower density in a woodland area of Northern England (Figures 3–7), with additional measurements on antler growth in a park stag (Figure 5).

Red deer clearly differ markedly in their growth and reproductive rates between high density conditions on hill-land and low density conditions in woodland. Whereas the effects of altitude and vegetation cannot be discounted as important influences on hill-land populations, there is good evidence that density alone can affect performance in this kind of habitat. Lower density populations tend to show higher weights of calves at birth, higher carcase weights in the next few age classes, higher pregnancy rates in milk hinds, and often with some pregnancies amongst yearling hinds; effects on older deer, especially hinds, are less obvious.

Figure 2 The growth rates of stags and hinds in two populations (one on hill-land, the other in woodland), as shown by the gralloched carcase weights of deer shot in the normal shooting seasons.

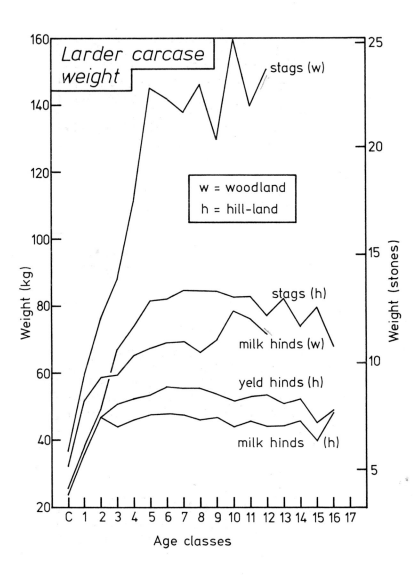

Figure 3 Changes in fertility and condition with age in stags and hinds in a hill-land population. (Condition is measured as a kidney fat index, ie weight of kidneys plus surrounding fat divided by weight of kidneys).

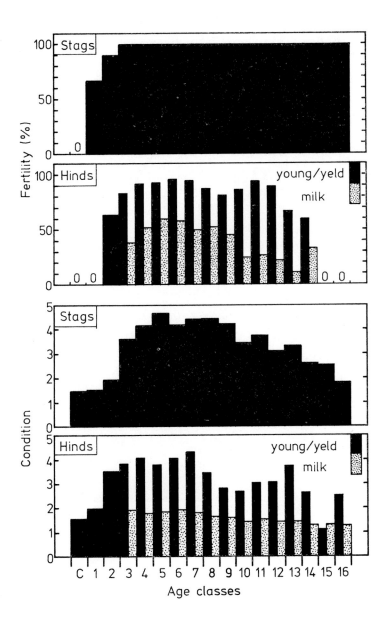

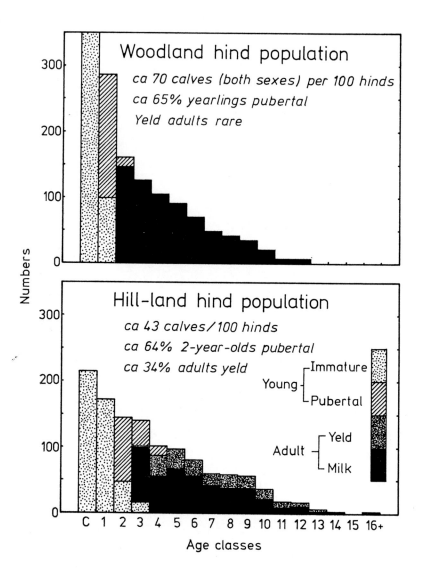

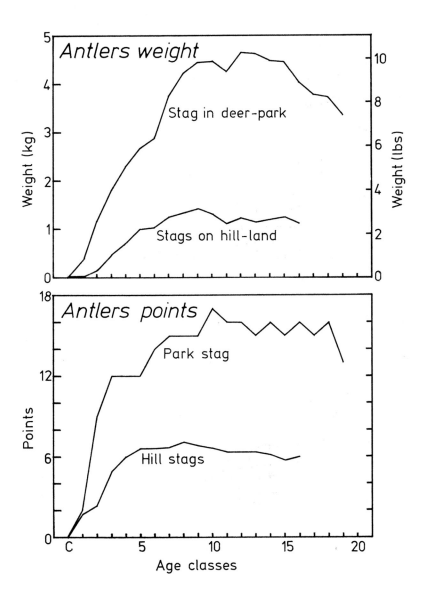

Changes with Age

The life of a red deer consists of three stages:

(i)   active growth and development, including sexual maturation (up to about 5 years);

(ii) high and relatively stable body weight, condition and reproductive efficiency (5 to 10 years);

(iii) progressive decline or senescence (11 years and above).

Stags and hinds differ in body size throughout their lives, although the differences are relatively small during the first year, increasing thereafter, especially after puberty (see Figure 2). On Scottish hill-land, stags are about 15 lb (6·8 kg) and hinds about 14 lb (6·4 kg) at birth, but as full-grown adults (5 to 10 years) stags are about 277 lb (126 kg) and hinds 193 lb (88 kg) in live weight. Growth rates are, of course, appreciably greater in woodland habitats.

Stags reach their maximum body weight a little later in life than hinds, ie about 9 years in stags compared with 7 years in hinds. Maximum condition (fatness) occurs a little earlier than maximum body weight in both sexes, ie 5–7 years in stags and 3–5 years in hinds (see Figure 3). Maximum antler size seems to be attained a little later than maximum body weight in stags (see Figure 5).

Sexual maturity (puberty) occurs at its earliest in yearlings of both sexes, that is to say at about 1 year 4 months, but this is affected by the growth rate of the animals, slow growth leading to late maturation. In woodland populations, most stags and hinds reach puberty as yearlings, and the adult hinds mostly breed every year. On Scottish hill-land, whereas most stags mature sexually as yearlings, the majority of hinds reach puberty as 2 year-olds, and a few even later, and appreciable proportions of the adult hinds have to rest from breeding every two or three years. As discussed elsewhere (see also Figures 3 and 4), a characteristic feature of red deer populations on Scottish hill-land is the existence of yeld hinds, ie adult hinds which failed to breed the previous year and which are now non-lactating, in good condition and with a high pregnancy rate.

The Annual Growth Pattern

The annual pattern of growth in red deer is determined primarily by seasonal changes in the quality of the available forage; the deer increase in body weight and condition during the annual period of vegetation growth, ie roughly from early April until late October on hill-land. By contrast, they lose weight and condition during the colder months, when the vegetation is declining in quality and availability, and when exposure increases the 'energy cost of living'.

However, other factors—especially reproduction—have their own effects on body weight and condition over the year in each class of deer. Stags reach their best in weight and condition by mid-September, just before the rut. During the rut, individual stags tend to remain in defence of their hinds for three or four weeks before relinquishing possession to younger beasts. This period of high activity and much-reduced food intake causes a dramatic loss in body weight and condition; an average stag loses about 15% in larder carcase weight and most of its discernible body fat. A similar amount of weight is lost over the winter. The fact that castrated stags attain their maximum body weight later in the autumn (as in yeld hinds) suggests that the rut, in effect, interrupts the growth pattern in stags.

Hinds in poor condition during early autumn do not become pregnant, and in consequence they do not lose as much weight and condition as those hinds which have become pregnant. During the calving season, therefore, there is little differ-ence in weight and condition between those hinds which have produced calves (milk hinds) and those which have not (yeld hinds). After this period, the yeld hinds gain in weight and condition faster, and continue to do so for a month or more longer, than the milk hinds. Yeld adult and milk hinds differ both in their average levels of body weight and condition, milk hinds being about 17% lighter than yeld hinds in mid-autumn, and at times of maximum and minimum weight and condition.

The slower and earlier cessation of growth in milk hinds reflect the effects of lactation. The differences between yeld adult and milk hinds during early autumn also affect their ovulation and pregnancy rates, since ovulation depends on body weight and condition. In most hill-land populations, yeld adult hinds achieve a pregnancy rate of over 90%, compared with about 50% in milk hinds; the latter may be appreciably higher in low density populations.

Lactation has a much bigger effect on the body weight and condition of hinds than does pregnancy, and it is only in the late stages of pregnancy that any direct effect on weight and condition can be detected.

The potential rate of population increase depends directly on the birth rate, which, in turn, depends on the age structure and reproductive capabilities of the female part of the population. Figure 4 shows these features in a woodland popu-lation and one on hill-land. As can be seen, the higher birth rate in the woodland population arises from the fact that most hinds become sexually mature as yearlings, and that virtually all adult hinds are milk. The lower birth rate in the hill-land population is due to a later age of puberty and to the high proportion of yeld adult hinds. It is of interest to note here the differences in age structure between these two populations, and the apparent paradox that there is a higher proportion of old animals in a hill-land population. This arises from the lower birth rate—which both affects and is affected by the age structure—and not from the fact that deer tend to live longer in this habitat.

Antler Size

Understandably enough, antler size is of special interest to sportsmen, and it is

25

lear that the antlers of hill stags are smaller in size, weight and number of points than those of woodland or parkland stags. Figure 5 shows the antler development ʋi one park stag (which lived for 19½ years) compared with those of stags in a hill-land population. In woodland, antlers of 7 to 10 lb (3 to 4·5 kg) a pair are fairly common, the biggest recent example known from a Scottish woodland weighing about 20 lb (9 kg). In eastern Europe, antlers can reach 26 lb (12 kg) or more. The relationship between antler size and body size in red deer, first studied over 50 years ago, is an example of disproportionate growth; increasing body weight produces a relatively greater increase in antler weight. While antler growth is partly controlled by age and condition, enhanced quality of summer feeding can bring dramatic increases in size.

Coat

Red deer have two moults each year; the red-brown summer coat is replaced by the darker grey-brown winter coat in October and November. The winter coat is shed over a comparatively long period of the spring, the new summer coat appearing throughout June, animals in poor condition being later than those in good condition. Condition also affects the quality of the coat, poorer animals having poorer coats, eg adult yeld hinds tend to have much thicker coats than do milk hinds. Observation and common sense interpretation of this and the other factors mentioned in this chapter provide a guide to managers of the performance and overall condition of the deer in their area.

The Yeld Hind

Although not shown on the graph of larder carcase weight (Figure 2), as there were insufficient measurements, yeld hinds in the woodland population tended to be lighter than milk hinds; the fact that on hill-land yeld hinds were heavier than milk hinds is shown quite clearly. The explanation for this lies in the question—'What are yeld hinds?'. Most of the yeld adult hinds on hill-land are those which have just recovered from the effects of an earlier pregnancy, because they did not regain sufficient condition to allow ovulation and conception whilst lactating. However, a small proportion of the yeld adult hinds are simply 'poor doers' which are incapable of breeding more than once every few years. Truly barren hinds are rare. So, on hill-land, the greater proportion of the yeld adult hinds are in the former type (in good condition). Some 'yeld hinds' are, of course, those which have recently lost their current calves and stopped lactating. In general, therefore, the high proportion of yeld adult hinds in hill-land populations is simply an expression of the responses of the deer to a poor and harsh environment. By contrast, in woodland habitats and deer parks there are few if any adult yeld hinds.

In shooting parlance 'yeld hinds' are all of those kinds of hinds which do not have calves at foot, ie including immature hinds and potential first-breeders. Examination of cull records in several areas of Scotland showed that some 30% or more of the 'yeld hinds' brought into the larders were immature hinds and those which had just reached puberty—possibly the cream of the future breeders.

Life-span

It is not easy to establish the theoretical maximum life-span for red deer. In practice, few animals reach 20 years of age in natural or even park populations, the average age at death being very much lower.

Mortality

Most natural mortality in calves and adults occurs from late winter to early spring. The main causes are a combination of under-nutrition, exposure, condition and old age. The deer most likely to die at this time of year are these in poorest condition during the autumn, namely the very old which also have worn teeth, the very young and those either 'ailing' or with injuries. Very few adult stags die during late autumn from injuries sustained during the rut. It is also rare for stags to die of 'natural causes' during the period that they have antlers in velvet; generally speaking, if they are in good enough condition to cast their antlers they are capable of surviving.

Deaths among hinds are commonest during late winter and early spring, but some, mostly first-breeders, die as a result of calving difficulties.

Deaths among calves during the calving season and a month or so afterwards are much more common and of considerable significance from the management point of view.

Apart from still-births, at least one important cause of calf mortality is failure or delay of lactation in the hind, especially in first-breeders. Predation by eagles and foxes is much less important than popularly supposed, though dead calves are taken as carrion. Losses of embryos by natural abortion or resorption appear to be comparatively infrequent but information on this is scant. If a hind is in good enough condition to become pregnant she can generally sustain the developing embryo.

The amount of natural mortality varies considerably from year to year and area to area. It is affected partly by the severity of winter, by the local pressure on the available forage and shelter and also by the selectivity of culling.

In an average year, even with a well-cropped stock, over-winter natural mortality rates of about 3% of adults and 10% of calves should be expected. In a very severe winter the corresponding rates could be as high as 15 to 20% of adults and 60 to 75% of calves, but probably not much higher. Being slow breeders and long-lived animals, red deer are not likely to experience severe fluctuations of population.

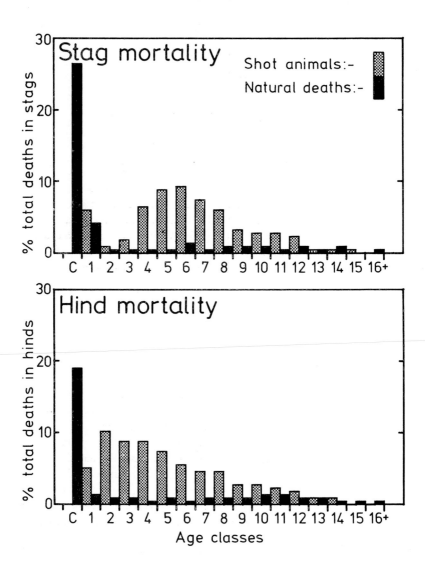

Figure 6 Patterns of mortality in one hill-land population, expressed for convenience as percentages of the total in each sex.

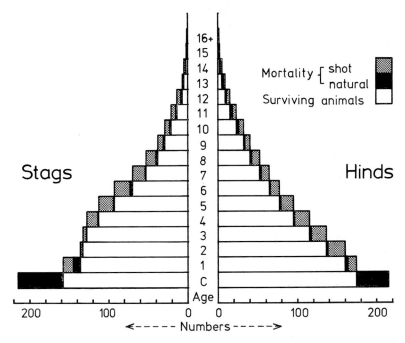

Figure 7 The sex and age structure of one hill-land population, showing the patterns of mortality. The unshaded sections show the post winter populations.

On present evidence, it seems that the average level of natural calf mortality is around 20 to 25%, with *half of this* during and immediately after the calving season and the rest during late winter to early spring. Therefore, an average birth rate of around 43 calves per 100 hinds becomes reduced to an equivalent recruitment rate of about 34 surviving calves per 100 hinds following a reasonable winter.

The natural mortality rate in calves is about 8 to 10 times that in yearlings. Whereas 50% of the calves found dead are males, the proportion of males is appreciably higher in dead yearlings. But the higher mortality of yearling stags than yearling hinds must have only a small effect on the overall proportion of stags and hinds entering the adult population.

Figure 6 gives results from one hill-land population and shows clearly the different patterns of mortality due to shooting and natural causes. Traditional shooting tends to select animals from the middle age classes, at maximum body size, whereas natural mortality affects mainly the very old and the very young. In this example, traditional shooting has been modified by the inclusion of some milk hinds and calves (compare patterns shown in Figure 7).

Chapter 5　Health and Well-being

While there is still much to be investigated regarding the incidence and possible effects of disease organisms (bacteria and viruses) and parasites on the health and well-being of Scottish red deer, present evidence suggests that these are of little consequence; the main environmental stresses faced by the deer are those of under-nutrition, exposure in winter and high stock density.

Diseases

Diseases that give concern in agriculture appear to be either absent or compara-tively rare in deer. Neither brucellosis nor 'foot and mouth' disease has ever been found in red deer. Leptospirosis is rare; louping-ill antibody has been found but deer show no visible symptoms. Some forms of TB have been discovered. It may be that more reliable information on the diseases affecting red deer will arise from deer farming and the recently introduced system of carcase inspection imposed by the importers of Scottish venison.

Parasites

A variety of small parasitic intestinal worms infests red deer but at levels generally below those causing poor health in domestic livestock.

While larger parasites are more common and more easily detected, there is little information on infestation levels or on their geographic distribution within Scotland. These include lung worms, two species of tapeworms (one present as the adult worm within the gut and the other present as the intermediate 'bladder-cyst' stage in the mesenteries), liver flukes, warble and nostril maggots, ticks, keds and one or two kinds of lice. Of these, the only ones likely to have detrimental effects on the health of the deer are lung worms, warble and nostril maggots, and ticks either because of high infestation levels or because of the times that they are present. High infestations of warble and nostril maggots could not come at a worse time since they emerge from the deer in spring when the animals are in poor condition. The characteristic 'stony livers' of high infestation levels of liver fluke are rare in red deer.

The traditional belief that deer move to higher ground during summer to avoid flies is unlikely to be the complete explanation. Deer respond to the presence of several kinds of insects, eg midges, clegs, head-flies, warble flies and nostril flies. Interference with normal feeding activity by continued annoyance from insects was observed at the experimental deer farm at Glensaugh where head-flies affected the feeding behaviour of stags. This situation would be more likely with confined deer than with those free-ranging on hill-land. The tendency for some areas of low-lying woodland to be abandoned by the deer in favour of high, open land during summer appears to be caused by a combination of escaping from insects and feeding preferences.

Chapter 6   Social Behaviour

A good deal is known about the ways in which red deer move around and distribute themselves on the open hill. Nonetheless there is still much that is not known about the factors involved and how they interact. Describing behaviour patterns is easier than explaining them. Two influences are involved:

(i)   social behaviour: that is the interaction between sexes and different age groups;

(ii)   habitat selection: that is seeking the most favourable conditions for food, shelter and security.

There has been a tendency for research to concentrate on one or other of these aspects whereas in reality both are involved.

Behaviour

The daily patterns of the movement of red deer can be partly explained as a precaution against predators, including man. On the open hill deer tend to be on the lower ground at night and the higher ground by day. On flat terrain cover is sought by day.

Deer are clearly social animals, occurring in groups, but with a marked tendency for stags and hinds with followers (calves and immature animals of both sexes) to live apart for most of the year. In addition, animals of the same class will move together to form groups and groups within groups; for instance, in late summer when hinds are at rest or undisturbed, the calves often congregate within the group for 'play'. When moving or disturbed, however, calves associate with their mothers. Yearling stags within a hind group will often band together. While the basic unit in a stag group is an individual stag, in a hind group it is generally a family of two or three animals. Within hind groups there are mature individuals that tend to initiate group activity.

There is considerable variation in the size of groups in any population of red deer. There are also seasonal changes and characteristic differences between areas and habitats in the average and maximum sizes of groups. Groups tend to be larger on open hill-land than in woodlands with a more marked separation of stags from hinds and their followers. Also, on hill-land, certain areas are characterised by larger groups. For example, on areas of rough, broken ground with poor or patchy vegetation, smaller groups can be expected than on smoother terrain with less variable vegetation. In some areas the largest groups can comprise no more than 30 deer; elsewhere, groups of as many as 500 or more may congregate. Apart from the tendency of deer to spill into unoccupied areas of favourable range, there is evidence of adjustments between groups, although much the same patterns will persist from year to year over given areas of range.

Habitat Selection

In deer forests that winter both sexes, the stag and hind grounds may be quite distinct with little or no overlap. Stag ground is mostly lower than hind ground, with both groups often found in the same valley. Stags generally select an area for shelter, with food a secondary factor, while the hinds' first preference is for quality of food. This is by no means the whole story, since stags are easier to attract to supplementary feeding. Certainly the diet of stags and hinds can differ in winter, with stags often taking more heather and the hinds more grass, but whether they deliberately seek out different feeding areas or merely respond to what is available is difficult to decide.

The result of ear-tagging experiments has demonstrated that while most hinds establish their home range close to their birth place, stags show more of an inclination to move away. This is to be expected because young stags usually leave the hind groups in their second autumn to join other stags and also because, in rutting, stags wander in search of hinds not always to return. During the rut it is the hinds that decide where they want to be and the master stag only attempts to restrict their movement so as to keep his group together.

A much clearer aspect of habitat selection or the distribution of deer is the effect of exposure. Where possible they choose the least exposed parts of their home range, especially for rest and rumination. During winter they favour the south facing rather than the colder north-facing slopes. The opposite applies in exceptionally hot summer conditions, when, by selecting the most windy locations, they avoid insects as well as the heat.

Disturbance

Deer vary in their response to disturbance from man between day and night, summer and winter and in different areas. They generally escape from disturbance by running away, but if their territory is restricted and movement is not possible deer appear to become more accustomed to people throughout the year. In winter, when deer are hungry, their need for food may overcome their normal attitude towards safety.

With the increased use of hill-land for a variety of human activities, the level of disturbance will continue to rise.

PART III MANAGEMENT

Chapter 7 Stock-taking

Objectives

Over the past two decades or so the economy of deer forests has become more dependent on venison sales and the interest in stags for stalking and for trophies has been supplemented by an interest in meat production. Populations of deer can be manipulated and cropped for either stalking or meat production and these objectives are best served by maintaining different populations in terms of sex-ratio and age-composition (see Figure 8). Present requirements, involving both objectives, lead to a compromise in terms of the composition of a managed population.

Stags and hinds are born in approximately equal numbers and the structure of a population in terms of sex and age is determined by the way in which mortality (natural and shot) affects each age class of stags and hinds.

Figure 7 shows the structure of one typical hill-land population in late summer after all calves are born and before any mortality occurs. For simplicity, the oldest deer (animals over 16 years of age were very rare) have been lumped together. Somewhat untypically this stock had almost the same numbers of adult stags and hinds, but otherwise showed a number of the more general properties to be expected in this kind of population:

(i) the birth rate of 43 calves to 100 hinds and a calf mortality rate of about 25% were representative of similar populations, as was the mortality due to shooting and natural causes. Natural mortality was experienced most heavily at either end of the age range in both sexes; this is best seen by comparing the relative widths of the black and white parts of each age column;

(ii) shooting (the shaded parts of each column) was spread over the middle age classes, extending more to the lower ages in hinds than in stags, eg the greatest numbers of stags shot were from the age range 5 to 7 year olds, and hinds from the 2 to 4 year olds. The difference in the shooting patterns of stags and hinds gave a different shape to the age structure of stags compared with hinds. Hind numbers fell steadily with age, whereas stag numbers declined slowly up to age 4 years and more quickly thereafter;

Figure 8 Diagrammatic representations of populations adjusted to suit different forms of production, showing sex/age structures and the forms of output. The calving rate used here is based on a typical hill-land population.

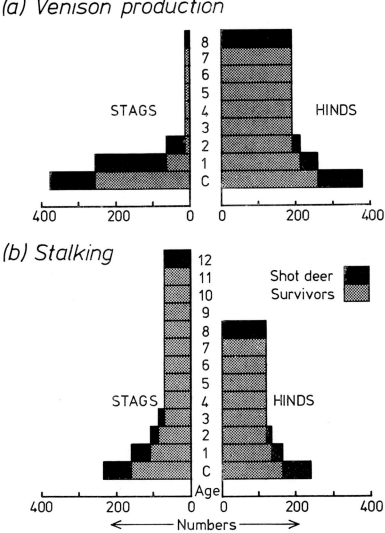

POPULATIONS MANAGED FOR:-

(a) Venison production

(b) Stalking

(iii)   a surprising fact about red deer populations is the comparatively low proportion of old animals; in the sample studied, which is typical in this respect,
half the population comprised animals of 3 years and below; only a little
over 5% of the total stock were 10 years and above;

(iv)   the pattern of natural mortality suggested that if shooting ceased the population would assume a more 'bell-shaped' age structure. After the initial
losses of calves and yearlings natural mortality would be comparatively low
until about 8 to 10 years, with increasing losses thereafter.

The study coincided with a period of shooting pressure above the traditional
level, but following the traditional kinds of selection milk hinds and their calves
were not shot. Knobbers shot in the hind season amounted to 5% of the total stag
cull; in other words, about 4% of the animals shot during the hind season were
actually young stags. This situation is not uncommon elsewhere in Scotland.

Taking account of the known age changes in body weight, condition, and
fertility of stags and hinds in this kind of population (see Figures 2 to 4), the
biological effects of changing the structure of the population for the production
of stags or meat can be examined.

Figure 8 illustrates how a similar population of 2000 adults aged 1 year and over
can be managed to increase either meat production or mature stags.

Figure 8a shows the effects of management to increase meat production. It is
assumed that mating failures will not occur at a ratio of four hinds per stag (a large
proportion of these stags being yearlings) and that hinds maintain their high
breeding performance up to 8 years old. It is also assumed that animals in poor
condition will be shot, thus preventing natural wastage.

Figure 8b shows a population managed to maximise the output of mature stags.
Aside from similar assumptions about the breeding efficiency of hinds and the
prevention of natural wastage, it is assumed that an equal sex ratio of adults gives
the best production rate for mature stags and that stags over 12 years would be of
little interest to sportsmen.

On paper these two populations would give different forms and rates of output
and they provide some pointers towards the uses and effects of selective cropping.

In population management the effects of density should also be considered. As
mentioned earlier, reducing the density must tend to favour increased performance
at the individual level, though on Scottish hill-land this increase might be quite
small. There is little information, at present, on which to base any estimates of
improvements at given levels of reduction. Moreover, improvements in individual
performance would have to be impossibly large to compensate for the overall loss
of production with a smaller population. The alternatives are, therefore, either a
high population density of relatively poor beasts giving a high total yield, or a
lower population of slightly better individuals resulting in a lower overall yield.

The Need to Count

It was probably difficult for the earlier stalkers, despite their knowledge of the habits of deer and their familiarity with the management of domestic livestock, to believe that a wild animal could be the subject of rational management practices. Deer then, as now, were often concealed by rough hill terrain and woodlands and moved on and off estates either seasonally or in response to the weather. Each deer forest was managed independently and the objectives and practices of management were strictly private.

Consequently there was no formal approach to stock assessment and the intensity of cropping, especially of hinds, was kept low. The deliberate under-cropping of deer was partly due to a fear of population depletion and partly due to the absence of a commercial venison market. It was known by the existence of yeld hinds that a fair proportion of hinds did not yield even one calf per year.

Initially, the main interest was in stags for stalking; it was mainly the larger ones that were taken, although some with poor antlers were also culled as 'rubbish'.

Hinds had little value other than as an attraction for the stags and for reproduction. Little attempt was made to control them. What hind cull there was concentrated on those without calves because these yielded the best mid-winter venison. Often immature hinds and first breeders, together with adults in good condition (most of them pregnant), were among those shot. The result was the best quality individuals from the population were selected, the stag cull being centred on the 5 to 7-year olds and the hind cull on the 2 to 4-year olds. These traditions, while preventing population depletion, led to rising densities of deer, high levels of natural mortality, more hinds than stags and higher proportions of young stags.

Those earlier traditions resulted from a lack of sound information on the properties of red deer populations, notably recruitment rates, and little incentive towards achieving more profitable levels of cropping, together with an unwillingness to seek and take advice. On the whole, these deficiencies no longer apply. The demand for deer-stalking continues and the market for venison has never been better.

It is in the national interest as well as that of each land-user that the animals are cropped effectively. Recent research relevant to cropping red deer has stimulated much interest among those involved in deer management, but implementation depends on regular stock assessment based on reliable counts.

The counting of red deer on open hill-land can be achieved and the term 'census' is not unreasonable. Apart from research on the island of Rhum, where counts could be checked, there is now a good deal of practical experience of monitoring population trends elsewhere in Scotland and accounting for them in terms of cropping rates. It is obviously more realistic to base changes in cropping practice on trends in numbers rather than on the results of a single count, mainly because of fluctuations in recruitment and mortality rates.

The Count

In 1952, the late Sir Frank Fraser Darling undertook a Deer Survey under the auspices of the Nature Conservancy. This was the first attempt at a country-wide census of deer in Scotland. Because of the limited size of the survey team it was unable to cover large blocks of terrain at any great speed, but by sampling different environments varying from heavily-stocked deer forest to marginal sheep ground, it provided a satisfactory basis for estimating the distribution and density of stocks of red deer. Indeed, the type of census now done by the Red Deer Commission (described below) evolved from the techniques first used by the Deer Survey.

Selection of Areas

For census purposes the Scottish deer range is divided into 45 areas or blocks which satisfy the following criteria:

Each area is sufficiently large to encompass the winter and summer ranges of both sexes with a perimeter of natural or man-made barriers which prevent any substantial movement in or out, for example, deer fences, sea and fresh water lochs, or the combination of road and railway often found running through a glen.

The area should be capable of division into sections which the census team can cover in a day and wherever possible these sections should be bounded by prominent physical features such as rivers, high ridges etc. The extent of each section will of course depend on the number of stalkers in the census team. Each experienced stalker will cover between 3000 acres (1215 hectares) and 5000 acres (2025 hectares) in a day.

The Aim

In counting deer there are three main objectives:

(i)   to count all the deer in the specified area;

(ii)   to classify them as accurately as possible into stags, hinds and calves, ie animals less than one year old;

(iii)   to carry out the count as rapidly as possible in order to minimise the risk of error arising from the movement of stock from one day to the next.

Timing

To achieve the above objectives the census should be:

(i)   at a time when deer are physically at a very low ebb (from late winter to early spring) with little or no day-to-day movement of the herds;

(ii)   when the weather is sufficiently severe to keep deer on lower ground. Complete snow cover is ideal as all the deer are on the lowest ground, substantially diminishing the area to be searched each day. Any deer remaining above the snow line are easily located and classified against the white background;

(iii)   when there is comparatively little disturbance on the hill from the end of the hind shooting in mid-February until early April when foxes are being dealt with and shepherds are going to the hill daily. During this period the differences in behaviour between the sexes are also most conspicuous.

The Team

The Red Deer Commission counting team consists of 8 to 10 experienced stalkers. Under favourable counting conditions up to 50,000 acres (20,250 hectares) can be covered in one day (10 men× 5000 acres).

Each stalker carries binoculars (normally 8× 30), a telescope (20 × –25 ×) and a small two-way radio. The binoculars are used to search the ground and locate deer, while the telescope is used for classification. The radio helps the stalker to maintain contact with his colleagues and to report movements of deer on to or off his particular area.

Each stalker has a 1:50,000 Ordnance Survey map with his own area and those of the stalkers adjacent to him clearly indicated. He records in a notebook all stags, hinds and calves he finds in the area allotted to him as well as the time and location of moving deer or deer likely to move. He also notes any easily recognisable beasts such as outstandingly good or bad heads, hummels or cripple beasts so that the same group can be identified if they are seen elsewhere.

Method

The methods vary, depending on the nature of the topography and the prevailing weather conditions.

On steep, open ground, particularly where one side of a glen is open to observation from the opposite side, counting can be carried out efficiently by a single stalker. He will not disturb the deer and there will be no risk of their moving and mixing with other deer. In broken ground or scrub woodland, stalkers should be employed in pairs, with one man to move the deer while the other counts and classifies them from a suitable vantage point. Scattered deer tend to herd when disturbed, but if they are moved quietly a satisfactory count can be obtained.

In severe weather, when deer tend to congregate in large herds on lower ground, stalkers are paired to check each other's figures.

Counting should be done in such a way that deer, if moved, tend to go on to ground already covered by the census team. This usually means working down or across the wind. A stalker working upwind tends to keep deer moving ahead of him so that they mix with deer not counted. This entails frequent re-counting of the same animals and separating them from the herds that they have joined.

The line on which each day's count ends is kept as short as possible to reduce the possibility of deer moving from the area already counted on to an area not yet covered or vice-versa. The finishing line for each day's count is the starting line on the following day and the same stalker carries on where he left off. Each stalker endeavours to maintain radio contact with the others of the team, particularly those working on ground adjacent to him. This eliminates much of the need to record times and movements of deer on the fringe of the areas and any doubts can be resolved on the spot.

When the day's count is completed, the stalkers meet as a group to report their figures. This evening session is essential as it affords the stalkers and the organiser an opportunity to compare notes and eliminate possible double counts. It is important that this discussion is held when all facts are fresh in the counters' minds. The census information is presented on a group by group basis and plotted on a scale 1:50,000 tracing of the count area. Totals for the count areas are published in the RDC Annual Reports.

Summary

(i) Red deer counts are conducted annually over parts of the range in Scotland.

(ii) Experience has enabled a standard counting procedure to be adopted.

(iii) Checks on accuracy usually mean checks on possible double counting with the elimination of small 'doubtful' groups.

(iv) No allowance can be made for deer overlooked by the team—in cold windy weather small groups can lie up unseen by even the most assiduous 'spyer'.

(v) No attempt is made to count deer in fenced woodlands—most of which harbour deer.

(vi) On open ground, with very good counting conditions, almost all the deer present will be seen and recorded.

(vii) With variable weather conditions, checks against possible double counting and the exclusion of woodland deer, the number recorded in any census is certainly fewer than are actually present and over-counts are extremely unlikely.

The Value of Census Material

Winter counts will give the detailed distribution of deer on their winter ranges and for an entire deer management area a total cull can be easily calculated, but individual estate culls are harder to determine as the estate may not have both summer and winter deer ranges.

Data from calf marking have proved a useful adjunct to counting by confirming that hind stocks are closely hefted to a relatively small total range. Tagging has also demonstrated that stags are capable of considerable seasonal movement. Therefore, while close relationships between the counted winter hind stocks and the hind culls are apparent, there is no link between winter counts of stags and local stag culls.

After issuing copies of the tracings of the census to the estates in the area, the Commission arrange meetings with owners, their representatives or their stalkers, who are always invited to accompany the RDC counting team over their own ground, to discuss the implications of the count on the management of deer in the area. This provides a forum for a general exchange of information and views. Accurate information on the number and age/sex composition of deer in any area is invaluable as a prerequisite for the management of deer units.

Chapter 8 Cropping: Theory and Practice

Selection

A great deal has been written and spoken about 'selective shooting'. It should be borne in mind that some forms of selection can be bad for the stock—for example, consistently taking the best can affect adversely the productivity of the stock. Selective shooting should have three distinct aims:

(i)   *weeding out,* ie eliminating the poor animal that does not contribute to the productivity of the stock;

(ii) *stock adjustment,* ie changing or maintaining the density, sex ratio, and age structure of the population to the kind of production required;

(iii) *achieving the desired crop.*

These aims are readily appreciated by agriculturalists, horticulturalists and foresters as applying to their own forms of production. Deer management differs from that of farm livestock in that selection and killing are combined as one process since poor stock cannot be fattened for marketing. There would be no problem in maximising the efficiency of deer management if the animals could be examined and handled first, and then killed or retained, but wild deer have to be assessed from a distance, and this assessment needs to take account of age and quality in relation to age. There is no easy way to gain the expertise necessary to grade deer at a distance. Visual comparison in small groups is the first essential, the poorest and best quality animals being the most easily identified. Depending on requirements, the good beast can be left and the poorest culled. With middle quality animals and single deer the exercise obviously becomes more difficult and it is only experience and observation which will provide the necessary skill in selection under these circumstances; in practical terms the best that can be achieved is to be 'right on average'. All deer brought into the larder should be carefully examined to assess age, condition and breeding status. The knowledge gained should then be applied to future selection.

What dies of natural causes each year is also a useful guide to weeding out, which should normally be concentrated on the very young and very old. Eradication of poor-looking hinds and calves should be a prime task and attention must always be paid to small body size. Potential can be recognised more easily in young stock and it is accepted that poor quality youngsters seldom develop into good adults.

The Crop

Since most managers on Scottish deer forests seek a high take-out of stags by stalking sportsmen and hinds as additional venison, there seems little advantage in attempting to attain an exact ratio of 1:1 between adult stags and hinds. A small excess of hinds is probably no disadvantage. Equal proportions of the two sexes are the best ratio for stag production where this is the sole objective of management, but the age structures of stags and hinds can be adjusted to suit the combined requirements of stalking and meat production. To increase the proportion of mature stags for sporting purposes, the main part of the stag cull should be taken from the younger classes, concentrating on the poorer quality. Maximising the breeding efficiency of the hind stock means eliminating the older and least efficient hinds. It is, therefore, good practice to take young stags and old hinds.

While the 'main crop' (ie best quality mature stags for the discerning sportsman and high quality carcases for the best venison) represents only part of the annual cull, a higher proportion of main crop in the total cull can be achieved ultimately by proper stock adjustment.

Hind cropping can be particularly difficult due mainly to short days and poor weather. Selection is not often a practical option if the desired numbers are to be killed. In fact, lack of selection or a completely random cull is preferable to the wrong selection of, say, yeld hinds. Because the former is likely to take out the same proportion of all grades of hinds, it will have no long term adverse effects on the fitness of the stock, although it will result in a slightly lower yield since some 'poor doers' are going to survive the cull. The old traditional yeld hind cull, however, will not only affect future production but will also result in the loss of an unacceptable number of the poor quality animals by natural mortality and result in a total loss in revenue. Wherever practicable, selection of the 'poor doer' should be the first aim in hind culling (Plate 1).

In certain circumstances, the behaviour of the hinds may aid the processes of weeding out and age adjustment, since the oldest, the poorest and the ones with the smallest calves tend to be first down on to the low ground. It is here on the low ground that much of the hind shooting effort should take place. As there is little likelihood of motherless calves surviving the winter, every effort should be made to take poor hinds and their calves.

A good deal of the stag shooting coincides with the middle stage of the rut (early October). Stags in possession of hinds at this time tend to be the best in the stock and shooting these can only lower the average age of the stags and gradually erode the potential of the stock. When possible it is probably wiser to start the shooting earlier, or to pay more attention to the groups of younger and poorer stags hanging around the rutting groups.

The Rifle

The choice of rifle for red deer stalking is very much a matter for the individual and it would be inappropriate to attempt to standardise the weaponry used. Bearing in mind the size of a large deer, however, there are certain statistics which provide the optimum combination of rifle and bullet for the job, namely a bullet of not less than 130 grains with a muzzle velocity of not less than 2750 ft (838 m) per second.

Ideally, the target should be at a distance of between 100 and 120 yards (91 m and 110 m) especially during a private stalk. It is accepted that the professional stalker may be called upon to shoot at a slightly greater distance, say during the hind cull, but stalking is not an excuse for attempts at 'fancy' shooting and the object of the stalk should be to despatch the animal painlessly and efficiently with the minimum margin of error.

The sport of deer stalking consists in the exertion and skill required in the approach to a firing position within range of the selected animal, by sportsmen who have made themselves proficient in the mastery of their rifle. To this code of conduct for all stalkers, professional or otherwise, must be added the rule that a wounded deer must be followed up, across estate marches if necessary, and that no other deer should be shot that day unless or until the wounded animal is despatched.

Chapter 9   **Carcases**

Recovery

The Scottish red deer range is so diverse in topography and private estates vary so much in size that no single method of carcase extraction can be universally suitable. Where deer stalking is only a part of a larger estate enterprise, the density of stalker/keepers, foresters and roads per square mile greatly exceeds those densities found in estates where deer stalking may be the primary land use.

The methods of carcase recovery must be determined by the scale and value of the enterprise and whether or not capital and running costs can be shared with other estate activities. In other words, roads, wheeled and tracked vehicles may service the forestry, agricultural and sporting aspects of estate management on a shared basis but could not be justified for a single enterprise. The methods of deer carcase recovery in current use fall into five categories.

(i)   *Dragging.* Pulling a deer by rope is back-breaking work and often restricts a stalker to kill only beside a road. Where a small estate shoots a small number of deer or where deer are shot close to an estate road the dragging method of extraction is commonly employed. It also limits the number of deer which can be stalked on a daily or seasonal basis. Moreover, carcase quality can suffer.

(ii)   *Pony extraction.* (Plate 2). This was the main method used on stalking estates from the late 1800s until the mid 20th century. Ponies were very much part of the stalking scene and the party often comprised the gentleman rifle, the stalker, ponymen and walking ghillies, together with one or more ponies. The ponymen and ponies followed the stalking party to the hill and waited at pre-arranged locations for a message from the stalker instructing them to proceed to collect a freshly killed stag or to move to another waiting place.

In the 19th century these ponies, common in the Highlands, were derived from the crofter's dual purpose ponies. Throughout the first half of the 20th century they were widely used on and by estates during the maintenance and building of roads, paths and grouse butts as well as for transporting sportsmen and game to and from the hill. Most stags were carried home strapped and balanced on deer saddles. On a small number of estates, stags were extracted on sledges drawn by pony. Similarly, hinds were carried, sledged or dragged from the hill.

(iii)   *Wheeled vehicles.* In the mid 20th century with labour and other costs rising, economies were made in staffing and this meant that on many estates pony and walking ghillies disappeared and the stalkers themselves operated a reduced number of ponies. More use was being made of ex-army 4-wheel drive vehicles and latterly a whole range of 3, 4, 6 and 8-wheeled vehicles for cross country use was developed.

(iv) *Tracked and track-laying vehicles.* Most of these vehicles were designed to overcome or traverse either deep snow or soft bog but they have been used successfully in a wide range of conditions. They are invaluable on mixed forestry, agricultural and sporting estates for tasks such as laying out new fence lines, winter feeding of stock, transport of shooting parties and extraction of game. They have proved particularly useful on estates which have a large hind cull but where the hind range is remote or difficult to reach because of deep snow. These vehicles, expensive to buy, all have their individual limitations.

(v) *Aerial extraction.* In this country there can be few large-scale deer culls which can justify the extraction of carcases by helicopter. However, New Zealand work has shown how effective this type of operation can be in a 'shoot-out' when deer are numerous and when ground access poses problems. Busy sportsmen, wishing a few days' stalking, have used helicopters to convey them from the airport of arrival to the sporting estate, and thence to the hill tops or to remote glens.

In short, hill transportation and carcase recovery is becoming more and more mechanised. On an estate basis, the degree and nature of mechanisation must depend on the economy of the estate and the scale of the stalking or sporting operation.

The almost exclusive stag cull of the past has now become a cropping operation in which stags and hinds are shot in equal proportion according to the recruitment rate. A greater degree of mechanisation helps to achieve the required cull in a more efficient manner.

The selection and purchase of recovery vehicles can best be done by the individual estates and by the stalkers who will use the equipment. Agents will be very willing to demonstrate their recovery equipment. Where the terrain is suitable it is recommended that vehicles should be used in association with two-way radios in order to direct the most efficient means of recovery.

Finally, the venison trade from producer to consumer is becoming more demanding for undamaged and clean carcases, and this requires good handling and the prompt recovery of culled deer. Mechanisation will play an even greater part in the future in improving hygiene and carcase quality.

Presentation

While the price of venison continues at a stable level, and the European market remains profitable, there are practical advantages in presenting carcases in the best possible condition for sale to the dealers. Abdominal or hindquarter shot deer, apart from the obvious suffering caused to the beast, will render considerable quantities of meat unsuitable for human consumption. As hygiene standards continue to rise, the well-presented carcase in good condition may show an additional financial benefit.

Deer visibly suffering from any unusual condition should only be presented to an approved export processor if accompanied by an explanatory note for the Veterinary Meat Inspectors appointed by the Department of Agriculture and Fisheries for Scotland.

It is not intended to describe the operation of gralloching and larder work in detail but it is considered that certain steps taken at this stage will result in definite improvements in the standard of carcases:

(i)   whenever possible the deer should be bled immediately after shooting with the head and neck kept below the level of the body;

(ii)   the gullet tube should be tied off before gralloching to prevent spillage into the body cavity;

(iii)   care should be taken to prevent any of the stomach contents leaking into the body cavity;

(iv)   the pluck should remain attached to the carcase or be placed, when cold, in a plastic bag and then associated with the appropriate carcase by a tag or tie. This is essential to meet the requirements of the export trade;

(v)   the cavity of a dirty, eg stomach shot, beast should be cleaned as soon as possible with disposable towelling; washing, especially under pressure, serves only to force bacteria into the cavity walls and accelerate contamination. And wet meat does not keep!

(vi)   a carcase should be dragged on to its side with care taken to avoid rolling; apart from the possibility of causing damage, dirt can more easily enter the body cavity. Opening the chest cavity is a matter of choice which often depends on weather conditions, but it can lead to the intrusion of dirt;

(vii)   *carcases should be taken off the hill as soon as possible after killing and hung in cool well-ventilated or refrigerated premises;* at all times the limbs should be kept apart to allow adequate circulation of air. Complete and careful removal of the back end is essential to a good carcase. For exports to West Germany, regulations are in force governing the time limit by which a carcase must be deposited in a larder or equivalent location.

Standard Carcase Weight

The weight used for larder or record purposes often differs by tradition from estate to estate.

While it may not be possible to bring into line the means by which carcase weights are arrived at for the Game Book, the only reliable standard weight is that of the skin-on carcase when it reaches the venison dealer, that is minus head, feet, pluck and kidney fat.

Ageing Techniques

A practical guide to age assessment is attached as Appendix A.

The Estate Larder

In the past, estate larders were designed or built to handle a certain number of stags stalked in the season. On the bigger estates, with a large cull, these buildings could be elaborate with all the conveniences of a hygienic slaughterhouse or butcher's shop. On the smaller estates, with a low cull, various sheds or byres were used to hang carcases.

As there is no current legislation governing the design of estate game stores, the following observations are for guidance only.

(i)   The working area of the larder should be large enough and the beams strong enough to handle and to hang two days' cull. There may be occasions when the game dealer is not able to uplift carcases daily.

(ii)   The building should be well ventilated and completely fly and vermin proof.

(iii)   The floor and walls should have a smooth finish, and capable of being washed down and thoroughly cleaned.

(iv)   The floor should be dished to a drain with an external trap and vent.

(v)   The larder should be served by running water and have a sink for hand-washing.

(vi)   Hanging rails and lifting pulleys are essential to aid handling.

(vii)   The volume of carcase throughput may justify the inclusion of a chill room. In this case, the working area will not be used for a hanging room so that floor space can be reduced accordingly.

(viii)   Management groups or several estates may join together in the erection of a central chill room and embark on a joint marketing scheme.

(ix)   Further information about larders, including those suitable for holding venison intended for export, can be obtained from the local District Veterinary Officer, Department of Agriculture and Fisheries for Scotland.

Metric Conversion Table—Pounds to Kilograms

The bold figures in the central column can be read as either pounds or kilos. Thus 1 lb=0·45 kilos or 1 kilo=2·20 lbs. For tens, move decimal point one place to the right, for hundreds two places, for thousands three places etc. Then convert higher quantities thus: 33 lbs=1·36 kilos+13·6 kilos=14·9 kilos.

Pounds		Kilograms
2·20	1	0·45
4·41	2	0·91
6·61	3	1·36
8·82	4	1·81
11·02	5	2·27
13·23	6	2·72
15·43	7	3·18
17·64	8	3·63
19·84	9	4·08

Plate 1. Selection for culling.

Plate 2. A carcase correctly loaded on a pony.

HEATHER (*CALLUNA VULGARIS*) RANGE REPRESENTATIVE OF EASTERN HEATH TYPE

Plate 3. Heather slopes well grazed by deer (Glenfiddich).

Plate 4. Heather slopes less heavily used by deer, with regenerating Scots pine (Rothiemurchus).

WET MOORLAND RANGE OF THE WESTERN TYPE

Plate 5.   Mixed *Molinia* (*M. caerulea*) and deer sedge (*Trichophorum cespitosum*) in October when forage is brown and dead (Wester Ross).

Plate 6.   Heather largely replaced by *Molinia* which in May still offers no new growth.

Plate 7.   A mixture of heather and *Molinia* in August when the latter, although still green, tends to be coarse and fibrous and is usually avoided by grazing animals (Glenfeshie).

Plate 8. Sward type grassland, dominated by bents (*Agrostis* species) and fescues (*Festuca* species) at 1000 ft (305m) being grazed by stags in June before moving to higher ground (Glenfeshie).

HIGH-LEVEL PASTURES, ABOVE THE TREE LINE, IN THE CENTRAL HIGHLANDS

Plate 9.　Snow lying in June. Above 2500 ft (762m) there is little growth until June or July and the grazing season lasts for only a few weeks.

Plate 10.　Grass sward on sheltered slopes along a burn at 3100 ft (945m) in late July (Cairngorms).

Plate 11.　Sparse grazing on lichen-rich (*Juncus trifidus*) heath in July (Cairngorms).

Plate 12. 'Flush' vegetation, dominated by the rush *Juncus acutiflorus* (foreground). Flushed areas provide a green 'bite' early in the year for deer; when the water supply is mineral-rich several useful forage species are found.

Plate 13. Juniper (*Juniperus communis*) shrubs give shelter and provide browse when other forage is covered by snow (Glenfeshie).

TYPES OF SOIL   Two profiles from the eastern range type.

Plate 14.   Soil of the *mor* type as commonly found under heather (*Calluna vulgaris*) in the eastern Grampians.

Plate 15.   Soil transitional to *mull* type bearing bents (*Agrostis* species), fescues (*Festuca* species) and *Nardus*; a soil that could readily develop into a true *mull* type or, at the other extreme, into a pronounced *mor* type, depending on the grazing and other treatments received.

TYPES OF SOIL   Two profiles from the western Highlands.

Plate 16.   A *mor* type peaty soil bearing *Molinia* with few other associated species.

Plate 17.   A soil of the *mull* type bearing close-grazed bent (*Agrostis* species)/fescue (*Festuca* species) grassland.

Plate 18. Heather (*Calluna vulgaris*), one of the most valuable forage plants on the hill, provides year-long grazing and browse. Frequent burning, or burning with a 'hot' fire, and subsequent heavy grazing can kill it. In the left foreground the well-drained and fertile *mull* soil enabled a bent (*Agrostis* species)/fescue (*Festuca* species) grass sward to develop producing useful grazing for much of the year; but on the wetter *mor* soil in the background *Molinia* became dominant providing useful grazing for only a short period in the spring.

Plate 19. An area improved for farm stock in Caithness where exploitation by red deer may also occur. In areas improved specifically for deer only hardy and persistent varieties of grasses and clovers capable of withstanding heavy and continuous grazing should be used.

Plate 20.   Shallow peat showing water erosion after heather burning during an exceptionally dry period with the result that the surface peat caught fire and vegetation failed to re-generate. After a few years the peat was completely removed by erosion leaving bare rock.

Plate 21.   Pressure on a deer fence.

FOREST DAMAGE

Plate 22.   Browsing (Fuinary).

Plate 23.   Bark stripping.

Chapter 10   **Range Management**

Red deer management often consists of little more than culling and some small-scale supplementary feeding. But it is equally important to consider the range, the forage, cover and shelter it produces, as this is the fundamental hill resource that sustains red deer along with other grazing animals.

An attempt should be made to manage the range wherever practicable, but even if management cannot be practised effectively the range resource should be understood by those who use it. Knowledge of the capability of range and of the consequences of using it in different ways may not necessarily lead to improvements in the animal crop, but such understanding can help to avoid making decisions that may turn out to be costly mistakes.

The term 'range' is a less familiar word in Scotland than in some other countries where it is used to describe extensive tracts of unfenced, and more or less natural, grazing land. 'Range' helps to get away from ideas implied by 'grazings', a term suggesting only one aspect of the complex structure that makes up Highland range; it also serves to emphasise that the approach to managing this system must be very different from that applicable to cultivated grasslands on good soils where intensive treatment, including stock control, is feasible.

This chapter is not, and indeed cannot be, a detailed guide to range management, but it does attempt broadly to outline the more important principles and to describe some practical problems in applying them to the use of land for wild red deer.

The Need for Range Management

A positive approach to range management is necessary for three main reasons:

(i)   to maintain the range in good condition throughout the year in order to provide for the different seasonal needs of animals for forage, cover and shelter;

(ii)   to enable different uses within the managed area to be harmonised, taking into account adjoining land likely to be affected by ranging deer;

(iii) to optimise output of the land in the long-term, whether for production of deer or for other aims of management.

The last requirement implies that the way the range is utilised should itself tend to improve the range for the desired purpose. Indeed, a fundamental principle of management is that, as far as possible, the productive capacity of the range should be sustained for long-term use without dependence on periodic and heavy inputs of capital. This requirement demands careful consideration of stocking rate, one of the principal tools of management.

Failure to think in range terms results in the long-term development of conditions that are simply consequences of animal management. Paradoxically this creates increasing difficulties in manipulating the range cheaply in ways that can best fit it to the needs of the animals themselves.

In order to maintain a healthy and flexible production system it is just as important to identify and interpret the signs that tell of range condition as it is to observe indicators of stock condition.

Range management is only partly a science. In practice it is also an art, depending heavily on field experience to interpret the signs and to understand how known principles relate to particular circumstances.

In brief, 'know your range'.

Basic Information Required

Whereas many different considerations affect range management decisions, basic knowledge required specifically about the range to enable proper management to be practised can be summarised as follows:

(i)   the distribution pattern of the different kinds of vegetation;

(ii)   the extent to which the vegetation is changing and where changes are taking place;

(iii)   the kind of vegetation that is beginning to replace existing types;

(iv)   approximate numbers of red deer and other grazing animals;

(v)   the seasonal use by deer of the range vegetation and the consequent grazing pressure, that is, the degree of forage utilisation in relation to the amount available.

Information in the first category (i) is often unique to a particular area and the range manager or stalker is generally more familiar with this feature than anyone else. Local knowledge of changes occurring in the vegetation (ii) and (iii) may also be considerable, but in this instance it is especially important to back-up practical range knowledge with scientific understanding of vegetation for reliable 'reading' of the range. Although it is certainly desirable to know how many deer use the range (iv), a range orientated approach places less reliance on knowing the absolute numbers of animals present, than on knowing the condition of the range and trends of change within it (v). Understanding *trend* in range condition, its causes and practical importance, is pre-eminently important in this approach.

Vegetation Types

Historically, much Highland range has developed from woodland. The area formerly supporting natural woodland, the *forest zone*, had an upper limit in the eastern and central Highlands of about 2000 ft (610 m). The potential tree-limit, and the *montane zone* above it, become progressively lower towards the west and north where, in exposed situations, the tree-limit may be close to sea-level.

Botanically, range vegetation is complex but it is usually quite easy to recognise the dominant plants. However, it should be remembered that other plants associated with the dominant species may be more important sources of forage than the dominants themselves. Five easily recognised categories of non-wooded range include most of the species found in Highland conditions and can be identified by the dominant plants present, and/or the circumstances affecting plant growth:

(i) heather (*Calluna vulgaris*) dominant vegetation (Plates 3 and 4), either of the eastern heath type or the wetter moorland type of the west;

(ii) wet moorland (Plates 5, 6 and 7) dominated by white grass (*Molinia caerulea*), deer sedge (*Trichophorum cespitosum*) or draw-moss (*Eriophorum vaginatum*);

(iii) sward-type grasslands (Plate 8) of bents (*Agrostis* species) and fescues (*Festuca* species) on the more fertile soils, and also mat-grass (*Nardus stricta*) 'species rich' pasture;

(iv) high level pastures situated well above the tree-line (Plates 9, 10 and 11) consisting mainly of grasses (including *Nardus*), sedges and dwarf shrubs;

(v) 'flushes' (Plate 12) with grasses, rushes, sedges and various broad-leaved herbs.

In addition, different kinds of woodland and shrub (eg juniper, Plate 13) may be found at low levels. Bracken (*Pteridium aquilinum*) which is common in some districts has been omitted but it is often associated with heather on the drier soils and with bent/fescue grasslands.

Soils

Red deer range can be divided broadly into two zones determined largely by rainfall. A line sweeping inland from the east coast of Sutherland, turning southward and continuing through Newtonmore and bisecting the Border west of Carter Bar marks the approximate division between the two types. To the north and west of this line peat soils predominate whereas to the east mineral soils, often with peaty humus in their surface layers, have developed in the lower rainfall conditions.

Although the underlying rock types, drainage and altitude all affect local conditions, the western range is characterised by extensive areas dominated by *Molinia* and deer sedge with varying amounts of heather, whereas in the eastern zone vigorously growing heather predominates and various sward-type grasslands are also more common.

Knowledge of soil conditions helps in predicting how the vegetation will change in response to policies of grazing, burning, drainage and other management. Screes and steep slopes apart, the simplest and most convenient classification is to recognise two broad soil categories (found in both the main rainfall areas) which can easily be related to the vegetation and which influence the behaviour and productivity of ruminant animals.

(i) '*Mor*' soils are very acid and usually peaty, or at least well-endowed with surface accumulations of undecomposed humus; the digging of a trench will show a 'profile' indicating very little evidence of vertical soil mixing. Examples of this type are found under pine forest and heather heaths or in wet peaty areas (Plates 14 and 16). Although drainage is not always seriously impeded, soils in this category are rather infertile and support few plant species.

(ii) '*Mull*' soils. In the other category, found mainly on the lower hill slopes and glen bottoms, there is typically more pronounced vertical mixing in the profile than in *mor* soils.

These so-called *mull*-type soils are also less acid and more fertile, usually containing more mineral matter and support more plant species of high grazing value (Plates 15 and 17). Such soils are found under many broad-leaved trees and also beneath the distinctive and often well-grazed bent/fescue grasslands where the nitrogen-fixing and nutritious white clover may also occur.

One of the most important differences between *mull** and *mor** soils is in the different responses to grazing shown by the vegetation that grows upon them (Plate 18).

Some Characteristics of Range Vegetation Types

The precise value of heather-dominated vegetation depends on what other plants are present and on the underlying soil. Although usually a *mor*, the soil under heather is sometimes of high enough inherent fertility to produce a *mull*-type humus when the heather is destroyed, so removing its influence on soil processes. On such relatively fertile soils, where the acid litter of heather itself maintains *mor* conditions, the heather can often be easily replaced by grassland of the nutritionally valuable bent/fescue type, especially when heavily grazed in the early years after burning.

Heather, nevertheless, is one of the most useful and versatile plants of the several

---

* Strictly, the terms *mull* and *mor* refer to the kinds of humus that form the surface layers of soils. However, as these are usually also useful indicators of fertility conditions and reflect a fairly sharp distinction between different soil categories along with the kinds of vegetation they support, the terms can be conveniently, if loosely, applied in practice to the soil and, by implication, to the whole soil/plant complex of a site.

dominant species. It provides grazing and browse at most times of the year as well as shelter and cover for both calves and mature animals. Above about 3000 ft (915 m) in the eastern and central Highlands, heather gives way to other dwarf shrubs and various kinds of grasses, including *Nardus* and sedges which at these elevations produce little forage except for the brief but important few weeks of summer grazing when deer are on the high ground. Little is known about the feeding value of these high-lying plant assemblages which provide good quality forage supporting calf growth and promoting the build-up of body condition in hinds and stags before the onset of winter.

Common range types on the poorer soils associated with heather (and often derived from heather-dominant vegetation in the middle and lower elevations) include *Molinia*, deer sedge and draw-moss, all of which are associated with mor-type soils. *Molinia* and deer sedge provide forage in the spring and early summer but rapid growth and increasing fibrousness soon discourage grazing, leaving a vast surplus relatively untapped. Both *Molinia* and deer sedge die back in the autumn and no green forage is provided until the emergence of new shoots in spring. Draw-moss, however, offers green forage for most of the year, the flowering shoots providing a particularly nutritious 'bite' in winter and early spring. 'Flushes' (Plate 12), particularly those influenced by mineral-rich water, are important early in the year when little fresh growth is available.

To a large extent bent/fescue grasslands are the 'key' to the quality of range though the total area on most Highland ranges is small, usually less than 5%. On low-lying fertile soils these grass swards can provide large quantities of high digestibility forage for long periods from spring to autumn. Sometimes bent/fescue grasslands on low ground are little-used by deer during summer when the animals are higher up, but make an important contribution early in the grazing year, providing recovery for stags, hinds and young stock after a long period of poor nutrition.

Changes in Range Vegetation: Burning and Grazing

Although a knowledge of the historical development of range vegetation can be useful in management, one must deal with the inherited range structure—essentially treeless albeit with some valuable woodland fragments still persisting, much unwisely and excessively burned, and containing large areas of little or no value for winter forage.

(a) *Burning* One of the most difficult management problems on most ranges is to strike the right balance for muirburn. Too frequent burning, especially in association with heavy grazing may eliminate or severely reduce heather, whereas too lenient a burning policy leads to the accumulation of large amounts of inflammable material that can fuel very hot damaging fires. Two basic rules should always be followed:

(i)   burn according to a predetermined plan and make sure that this is adhered to by applying effective control measures;

(ii)   err towards the conservative use of fire, except where it can be used deliberately to change existing vegetation to a type of greater permanent grazing value, as on the more fertile *mull*-type soils.

Vegetation changes from one kind to another because the component species respond differently to whatever treatments are applied. The simplest way of predicting vegetation changes is to recognise that plants with over-wintering buds disposed above the surface of the soil—for example heather or juniper—are sensitive to the effects of grazing and burning. Heather does, of course, sprout readily from the base of the plant when top growth is destroyed; but when this happens too frequently the plant is weakened and dominance is taken over by other species.

In a contrasting habit of growth the over-wintering buds of some species are located on the soil surface or beneath it, for instance, most grasses, sedges, rushes, blaeberry (*Vaccinium myrtillus*) and, notably, bracken. Plants of this type gain some protection from grazing and burning. They tend to increase in abundance where grazing is heavy and where burning is either too frequent or the fire too hot to enable heather to survive or to maintain its vigour. The particular species that become dominant depend largely on altitude and soil condition (eg *mull* or *mor*, wet or free-draining) as well as on grazing, but a good example of this principle of differential responses of species to imposed treatments is shown by the spread of bracken into heather vegetation. Bracken advance is often particularly rapid after a fire. Other examples are found on wet ground where *Molinia*, draw-moss, deer sedge and heath rush (*Juncus squarrosus*) are common constituents of heather vegetation and these species tend to become more abundant as the vigour of heather diminishes. Similarly, as already explained, at the drier and more fertile end of the soil spectrum, where bent and fescue grasses occur within the heather, a close-knit grass sward may develop as a result of burning and grazing.

(b) *Grazing*   The effects of fire are accentuated by heavy grazing which, with burning, interacts to produce changes in vegetation: the results are usually difficult to identify as separate pressures over the range as a whole.

On the more fertile *mull* soils the sward-forming grasslands derived from heather provide forage during a large part of the year. By contrast, on the less fertile *mor* soils, including large tracts of wet peaty range, heavy use produces more open vegetation that contains an abundance of mosses, deer sedge, heath rush and other species, many of which, unlike the heather they replace, are of grazing value only during restricted periods of the year and some of them are entirely useless for winter grazing. Moreover, lacking the close-knit sod found on sward-type grasslands, this range cannot carry large concentrations of animals without causing significant disturbance to the surface.

One of the most important aspects of range management is the care of areas where heather dominates. The vegetation of many ranges now seems to be relatively stable, although degraded in the sense that opportunities for improvement by low-cost management have been reduced by a long history of over-use. However, large areas still remain where judicious management can maintain, and possibly improve, range values. Many such areas are still predominantly heather-covered and therefore future effects of burning and grazing upon them need special consideration in framing management policies.

Stocking Rate and Mixed Stocking

The overall stocking rate and its effects on grazing pressure is of vital importance. For example, bent/fescue grass swards on *mull* soils can sustain high stocking rates during the growing season between May and September, especially if the soil is of high enough fertility to support white clover. Indeed, the heavy grazing pressures that these swards attract in this period are essential for maintaining their productivity and nutritional value. In fact, where the only grazing animals present are red deer, summer grazing on wintering ground may be too light to maintain bent/fescue patches in optimum condition, or even to maintain grass at all on these areas.

Heavy grazing pressures during the growing season can be effective in maintaining several types of non-wooded range in relatively good order and they can also create conditions, for example on several kinds of vegetation on *mor*-type soils, that reduce the need for frequent muirburn. In general, heavy grazing produces the most beneficial effects when it is restricted to certain limited periods of the year, but such precision in timing can rarely be attained deliberately by management on open range. Although heavy grazing at the right time and in the right place is a potent factor in range improvement, sustained heavy pressure can be very damaging.

Heavy and continuous pressure on the lower slopes during winter and spring depresses the growth of plants in the period before calving and leads to the impairment of heather—often in areas where its vigorous growth is so valuable in snow conditions.

On *mor* soils, where plants available for replacing heather give very restricted seasonal grazing with little to offer during the winter, the loss of heather is clearly a form of range deterioration, a condition that occurs extensively in the west.

The different grazing habits of red deer, sheep and cattle provide opportunities for exploiting the merits of each species of animal for good range management. In certain circumstances the presence of domestic stock may justify the use of fencing and grazing improvement techniques on limited areas of range, establishing local conditions from which deer may also benefit (Plate 19). With open-range grazing mixed stocking in summer can be advantageous, resulting in a more balanced use of forage. **But it should be remembered that the effects of a** high overall stocking rate cannot be absorbed simply through the different dietary preferences among the various animal species. Moreover, at high stocking rates less forage is carried into winter and, during this period, a highly competitive situation can arise for the limited forage available.

The optimum balance of advantage between over-use and under-use of range is not easy to determine but observations over a period of years, especially on ranges used during autumn, winter and spring, should indicate whether or not stocking rates should be adjusted. As in the case of burning, erring in the direction of under-use will maintain a better and more flexible range than persistent over-use, which produces deleterious and irreversible effects.

Carrying Capacity

Many managers instinctively feel that, using existing knowledge, there should be a straightforward way of arriving at the number of deer that represent the carrying capacity of a range. In practice, it is rarely possible to make categorical statements about range carrying capacity in terms of actual numbers of deer because so much depends on what the manager is trying to achieve, the kind and extent of management inputs he is prepared to apply and the degree of competition with other land uses that can be accepted. However, in attempting to evaluate carrying capacity, three main criteria can be considered:

(i) *animal criteria* concerning performance in terms of body weight, age of first calving, calving rate, survival, growth, development and winter mortality;

(ii) *range criteria* concerning condition of the range, grazing pressure and trends of change;

(iii) competition with other land uses or with aesthetic range values.

Although important, especially in certain areas, the last criteria involves issues beyond the scope of technical range management. While the animal and range criteria have to be considered together, it should be borne in mind that the links between them may not always be apparent. Overall, Highland range is of poor quality and a very considerable degree of improvement in the nutritional quality of the forage is likely to be necessary to upgrade most aspects of deer 'performance'. The availability of winter forage is one important factor that imposes a limitation on acceptable stocking rates: the size of the population is determined not so much by the extent of the summer range but rather by the available wintering facilities.

Evidence from 'reading the range' will indicate what trends are likely to contribute towards maintaining the existing system and what changes will be detrimental to it. This type of evidence, along with scientific data on aspects of animal and range biology, can greatly help the manager or owner to establish if his stated objectives are capable of practical achievement, ie by maintaining the *status quo*, allowing animal numbers to increase, or acting to reduce numbers. Managers are advised to seek assistance if an accurate scientific assessment of the range is considered desirable.

Tools of Range Management

The importance of grazing and muirburn as management tools has already been emphasised: other practices such as land drainage and bracken eradication are all complementary to grazing because of their direct effects on the range and because of the animals' reactions to resulting changes in range structure.

Similarly, liming, fertiliser application and/or seeding are other techniques that can be employed in localised areas, either specifically for deer, or as part of an associated farming enterprise. All these techniques may be useful for encouraging changes in deer grazing habits or, if extensive enough, for helping to improve deer nutrition for better reproductive performance and growth. This latter kind of radical improvement, however, is capital intensive and consequently its application is limited.

A vital point about range fertilisation is that neither lime nor fertiliser applications will give much benefit unless the areas selected for treatment contain plants that can readily respond to the better soil conditions to be created. Such responsive plants are usually found on *mull* areas which are often suitable subjects for improvement. Additionally, heavy grazing is usually required to encourage the growth of improved swards that the lime/fertiliser treatments make possible. Sometimes the area of improvable land can be extended by treating *mor* areas, but these will almost certainly require seeding along with the other treatments. The problem of range reversion is often worse on these soils than on *mull* soils that have been simply treated with lime and fertilisers. Unfortunately, *mor* soils (along with wet soils of any type) are particularly susceptible to eventual invasion by plants of poor grazing value as a result of sustained heavy grazing that successful land improvement may attract. To be realistic, it must be accepted that the problem of maintaining improved areas cannot be satisfactorily overcome except by fencing and stock control, a step towards intensification that is unlikely to be justified in normal deer range conditions.

Little progress has been made so far in the integration of deer management with forestry and agriculture. In fact the strategic use of woodland blocks along with agricultural developments needs much closer study before the potential of integrated usage can be realised for promoting the control of deer behaviour and performance without adversely affecting forestry and farming. However, the introduction of shelter belts, fenced at first, until they get under way, should be considered wherever practicable.

Management Planning

Information about range characteristics can clearly be used to assess the existing state of the range and to facilitate future decision-making on actions necessary for maintaining condition and output. It can help in deciding, for example, where forest blocks should be situated, what the likely effects on deer will be if sections of range are allotted for forestry and farming and what consequences are likely to follow greater stock concentrations on any part of the range.

A large-scale map showing contours is desirable as a base for recording the pattern of vegetation, as indicated by the dominant plants, and for the location of *mull* soil areas. Summer and winter ranges should be delineated and a rough indication of grazing pressures given by 'scoring' the range into zones on a convenient scale of values from 1 to 3 or 1 to 5, 1 representing light grazing pressure and 3 or 5 heavy pressure. It is also possible to indicate the changing status of the range by marking areas to show:

(i)   those of particular sensitivity where soil erosion is likely to occur (Plate 20);

(ii) where the vegetation is apparently stable;

(iii) where vegetation is evidently changing from one kind to another; the 'direction' of change being indicated by a plus (+) sign for development towards woodland or scrub (including heather) and a minus (−) sign for development in the opposite 'direction' towards grassland or other plant associations that replace heavily used woodland or heather.

Simple maps of this kind, carefully maintained, can be used to record much more information including eg drainage conditions and burning treatments. It is important, therefore, to make observations and to record them in such a way that they can be set alongside information about numbers of animals, their daily and seasonal movements and other habits. This kind of recording can help to alert all concerned as to what may be happening on the range and to stimulate a more informed approach to overall management of the entire system of which the red deer is only one component.

Finally, field observation and information recording make an effective dialogue more likely between those directly involved in management and those whose task it is to understand scientifically the principles affecting the range economy.

Chapter 11   Deer Fencing

The Problem of Fencing against Red Deer

In 1979 there was in existence well over 3000 miles (4830 km) of deer fencing in Scotland, two-thirds of which was on Forestry Commission land. The annual cost of erection and maintenance was around £500,000.

Although most deer fencing is carried out by farming and forestry interests, the deer manager should also consider the provision of fencing for better management of his herd or as a means of reducing marauding and killing out of season (Plate 21).

Much of the deer fencing erected since the Second World War was of poor construction and workmanship and many forestry plantations of exotic conifers have a permanent population of red deer that are now hefted to a woodland environment. If the blocks are big enough such deer are lost from the hill herds and from the sport of stalking and cease to be a source of estate revenue. The damage done by red deer in some plantations is often as spectacular as it is economically disastrous (Plates 22 and 23.) Deer are also able to raid farm crops from woodland if the only barrier is a standard stock fence.

Some fencing is erected as a deterrent rather than as a barrier, but this chapter will refer only to fences which are expected to give a useful life of some twenty years and are thought to be the best possible barrier to access by deer.

When considering the erection of a fence it should be remembered that situations can alter with time. For example, if trees are planted on ground with vegetation of little attraction for deer, their interest in gaining access may be minimal. Ten years later the trees will give dense shelter and prove highly attractive. The enclosure of traditional deer winter grazings will result in increasing pressure on the land as the same number of deer are competing for a smaller acreage. Thus, where a cheap fencing option is chosen in the first instance, the costs incurred in later replacement may be exorbitant.

Planning the Fence

At the initial stage the possible cost of fence construction will be balanced against the probable benefits and considerations such as:

What will be the effect on the movement of deer (especially in severe weather) and on their ability to find shelter and grazing on the land remaining to them and most importantly what, if any, reduction in population should be effected when the fence is closed?

Moreover, the effect on any farm stock involved must be considered.

The Red Deer Commission are consulted by the Forestry Commission on all forestry developments which affect deer. They are also prepared to give advice prior to the completion of proposals or to call a meeting of the interested parties in order that views may be exchanged. It can be very expensive to alter the line of a fence after it has already been erected.

The second stage in planning will involve setting out the actual line of the fence on the ground and plotting its outline on a large-scale map. At this stage local knowledge should be sought. Stalkers, shepherds and farmers who know the ground are best able to advise on snowdrifting and on which burns are liable to excessive flooding.

Attention should be paid to the following general rules:

(i)   fencing *along* a contour on steep ground should be avoided if deer will be approaching on the *higher side*. It may be wiser to enclose some unusable higher ground to take the fence across a flatter top. On steep slopes deer find it easier to jump into the enclosure. Moreover, boulder or snow slides are liable to break the fence;

(ii)   burns should be crossed where there is a hard bottom and an easy approach on either bank;

(iii)   where there is a choice, the fence line should be over *convex* topography or flat areas. Hollows should be avoided. Snow is more likely to blow clear where wind speed is steady or accelerates to cross a rise;

(iv)   thin soils over rock outcrop, peat hags with standing water and excessively uneven ground should be avoided;

(v)   if the fence bounds part of an existing wood there are two options: either it should be kept some way from the woodland edge to avoid snowdrifts or located inside the existing woodland (especially if this is of Scots pine or larch) at a stage that will not suffer bark stripping. Some woodland accessible to deer for shelter may well reduce pressure on the new fence;

(vi)   the fence line should be kept several feet back from stone walls where drifts are liable to form in times of storm;

(vii)   excessively long perimeters without break or sub-divisions should be avoided. Where a 3700 acre (1500 hectares) enclosure may be acceptable in an area of low deer pressure, a block of 1200 acres (500 hectares) may lead to trouble in a highly-stocked deer forest;

(viii) if deer are to be given access to lower ground, suitable downfalls should be provided and the fence planned to channel into them. Most natural gullies make excellent downfalls as they can often be left as deciduous woodland for amenity.

Unsatisfactory Specifications

The earliest deer fences erected by landowners were often of a very high standard with no expense spared. Posts were of galvanised steel drilled for up to eleven plain wires that were tensioned on patent winders at the metal strainers.

Deer fences erected in the post-war period attempted to copy these, using timber posts and strainers but they proved to be only a barrier in a low ground situation where frequent inspection and maintenance was possible; one loose or broken wire was enough to allow access by deer. In practice the standard of maintenance required was seldom achieved and it was very largely such fences that were penetrated by deer over the last twenty years. Early alternatives to the wire fence were those of diagonal mesh sheep netting or a combination of this type with rabbit netting, but it was found that a gauge suitable for sheep was not strong enough to keep out red deer.

Gauges of *less* than 14 for the top netting are *not* recommended. Where rabbit netting is used on the lower half it is a mistake to hang it on two or three plain wires. Four is about the minimum and five even better, otherwise deer can rip off the netting and get through between the line wires.

Another unsatisfactory option is the heightening of a stone dyke with wires or netting. It is only a matter of time before the deer knock out coping stones to gain access.

Perhaps the most disappointing development in recent years has been the wide use of patent clip fasteners for fixing netting or rylock to plain wires. This is not a reference to the spiral lashing rods which are excellent for use with rylock or weld-mesh netting, but to the small clips which are bent round the wire using a special tool. Bending the steel clips opens up the galvanising and at best about five years' life can be expected before they rust. When rusted, the bared clip allows electrolytic action to destroy the galvanising on any wire in contact with it. Before long netting and supporting wires are all showing rusted areas. Consequently, the fence loses much of its effective life and is not strong enough to hold netting against drifting snow or pressure from desperate deer.

Timber Materials

POSTS or STAKES. The leverage exerted on a 6 ft (1·8 m) high fence is twice that on a normal stock fence and therefore posts must be both stronger and driven more deeply into the ground. On firm ground the minimum length should be

$8\frac{1}{2}$ ft (2·6 m) and the top not less than $3'' \times 3''$ (76 mm $\times$ 76 mm), or $3''$ diameter (76 mm) in a round stake. The length must be increased to 9 ft (2·7 m) on soft ground or even 10 ft (3 m) in peat. Larch cut from heartwood is adequate for wet ground but has a short life on dry mineral soils where treated pine is best, if creosoted either by hot dipping or the pressure/vacuum process. The latter method can also be used with copper-chrome-arsenate (C.C.A.) chemicals. Both will give equal service life to the timber but creosote does increase damage to posts in the event of a ground fire. C.C.A. chemical treatment reduces inflammability by some 10%.

STRAINERS should be at least of length $10\frac{1}{2}$ ft (3·2 m) or $11\frac{1}{2}$ ft (3·4 m) in peat with a minimum top diameter of $8''$ (20 cm).

STAYS should be 10 ft (3·0 m) by $4''$ (10 cm).

Too many fences are erected with posts insufficiently driven; a reversed post instead of a stay is useless. Strainers should always be reinforced at ground level with a breast board unless they are driven in by a mechanical post driver. In peat the board has to be much larger than in firm ground. Timber treated by a preservation process when still green and full of sap will only take a surface impregnation, which is costly and inefficient. C.C.A. processes are subject to British Standards specification and the appropriate treatment certificate should be demanded. Preferably, materials should be obtained from a supplier who holds adequate stocks of treated fencing. Timber cut to order will need at least three months to dry before treatment is applied.

Metal Materials

LINE WIRES. Either no. 8 gauge mild steel or 10 or 12 gauge spring steel, galvanised to an accepted standard, is recommended. Spring steel has the advantage of greater strength and maintains better tension but calls for more skilled erection and the use of specialised tools. Forestry Commission Record No. 80 is recommended as a good general guide on fencing methods, particularly when high tensile wire is used.

DIAGONAL NETTING should be galvanised No. 14 gauge with a 4 in (10 cm) mesh. It should also have a centre strand. Although making an acceptable fence, diagonal netting is more liable to hold snow than rylock or weldmesh.

HINGED JOINT and RYLOCK type NETTING, galvanised pattern C6/90/30 medium grade field netting, is sufficient if only deer are involved. Where sheep are likely to be encountered, the bottom half of the deer fence should be upgraded to C8/80/15.

WELDED MESH NETTING is an alternative to the locked or hinged joint type. C6/90/30 FF3 for the top and C8/80/15 FF1 for the bottom is recommended.

PATENT DEER NETTING is marketed under various trade names. It is an important netting made specifically for deer, one height for roe and one of 6 ft 8 in (2·0 m) for red deer. There are 17 line wires of spring steel with verticals of mild steel wire at 12 in (30 cm) spacing. A high standard of galvanising is claimed for this netting which can be erected in one piece and tensioned to a considerable strain.

RABBIT NETTING, when used in deer country, should be 42 in (1050 mm) in width with 1¼ in (31 mm) mesh and a gauge of 18—6 in (15 cm) should be buried.

GENERAL. Two piece netting fences joined at a central line wire have two advantages. Firstly, they allow more flexibility for combining different mesh sizes according to the needs of the situation.

Secondly, if fencing has to be lowered to drive out deer, it is much easier to fold down the top half of a long length of two piece netting.

It is usually the bottom section of the fence that will suffer the greatest pressure from deer or other stock and so it should be of a higher specification. For the same reason several line wires are required to back up rabbit netting.

Forest Record No. 80, while otherwise an excellent guide, contains several recommendations that in the light of experience might be revised namely:

(i)   the use of patent netting clips;

(ii)   stakes or posts of less than 8½ ft (2·6 m);

(iii) the need for only 3 line wires to back 3 ft (0·9 m) high rabbit netting;

(iv)   post spacing that is too far apart for most hill situations.

When erecting one piece patent deer netting it is a mistake to fit each of the 17 line wires with a separate ratchet. It is better to make a stretcher bar with butterfly clips to apply tension to the netting which should then be nailed at the strainers. Provided that the latter are properly sunk and stayed the netting will remain well tensioned without the need of ratchets. The three backing line wires do, however, require to be tensioned on ratchets.

Weak Points

The effectiveness of any deer fence depends entirely on how well any weak points are dealt with. If there is an unguarded weakness the deer will find it and enter. The aim of the fencer must be to eliminate such a possibility. This aspect of deer fencing should be given separate consideration at both planning and erection stages when each danger point should be located, and stringent specifications be laid down with the contractor.

The following normally constitute weak points in any fence:

DITCHES crossing the fenceline. Deer will enlarge these with their feet to gain access. To prevent this happening the sides have to be piled with treated timber and in the case of a large ditch the entire cross-section may have to be boxed.

BURNS AND RIVERS must always be hung with watergates. Their purpose is to provide a barrier to entry at varying water levels. Above flood height should be netted between two strainers sunk at either side. Just above flood level a pole should be fixed and from it the watergate hung on short lengths of chain—wire should not be used since it invariably twists and the gate ends jam in the 'UP' position. The watergate should be of substantial construction, preferably weighted by a heavy sleeper. Where the direction of flow is into the enclosure, barbed wire should be nailed along the bottom and edges to deter deer from pushing under it. With the direction of flow coming out of the enclosure stops should be introduced to prevent the gate being pushed backwards. Unless there are natural rock sides to the watergate a firm straight side, made with timber piling, is essential. Deer will soon dig out a bank beside a watergate. If they do not, nature will, after a few floods.

GROUND LEVEL GAPS should *never* be made up with sticks, stones or turves which will soon be raked out by deer. There are two options:

(i)   such gaps should be made up with additional netting and posts;

(ii)   fencing should be pulled down using a ground anchor or large boulder. Ground anchors are now available in the form of patent discs that are screwed into the ground with a special tool. They have a length of wire attached to them and this ties down the fencing to close up the gap. There are two sizes of disc, the larger being for soft ground. Discs will take a strain of up to 600 lb (272 kg). In very spongy peat probably the only recourse is a large boulder.

ROCK OUTCROPS. Where rock outcrops are unavoidable, galvanised steel posts should be cemented into the rock. If long spaces are left between posts to economise on costs, the intervening fencing should be heavily weighted by tying large stones to the bottom wire.

SNOWDRIFTS. Wherever a fence is prone to drifting its height should be increased appropriately. Following completion, fences should be inspected after snowstorms to see if there are additional places which require heightening. It may also be necessary to strengthen the fence by putting a stay to each post in areas subject to severe drifting. These can be made of stout rails nailed to the top of the existing posts and to a shorter fence stob driven down to ground level.

Access and Jump-outs

VEHICLE ACCESS. Where frequent passage of vehicles is present a grid will be needed. This can be of similar construction to a cattle grid but must be longer 16 ft (4·9 m) is the minimum width to stop deer jumping across. The grid must also be deeper to ensure that it is not blocked by heavy snowfalls.

GATES should be specially constructed to full deer fence height. The top hinge should be turned upside down to prevent the gate being lifted off and a chain and padlock provided. An ordinary field gate with movable bars is inadequate as invariably the bars are left off or break.

STYLES. It is good practice to use these rather than gates, which are often left open to provide passage for hill-walkers, stalkers or sportsmen. Styles can easily be made from four fence posts with lengths of rail for steps. The latter should be supported with fence wire nailed over them.

Where sportsmen or shepherds are to use the style a dog pass should be incorporated. The captive type which drops back into place under its own weight is recommended.

JUMP-OUTS are perhaps one of the most important provisions for any deer fence. However good the fence, deer will one day break in during a storm or other mishap. Before they colonise the plantation an opportunity usually arises to encourage them to leave. They may even wish to do so of their own accord. Accordingly, it is important to provide adequate facilities to allow them to jump the fence. A height of about 3 ft (0·9 m) on the inside is recommended, the normal height being retained on the outside. Exit jumps were formerly constructed with timber, stones or turf or a combination of all three. These jumps were seldom efficient as they betrayed their artificial origin and the deer were shy to use them. By far the cheapest and best method of jump-out construction is to level a section of any slight rise in ground level occurring along the fenceline. This can be done with a back-end digger or a light bulldozer. A hard edge of 3 ft (0·9 m) is cut along the proposed line and the fence is then erected at the base of the cutting to provide a natural rise on the inside of the enclosure. Deer will then walk up the slope and jump the fence. Jump-outs should not be located where drifting is likely to occur as the embankment may snow up on the outside of the fence.

Workmanship

It is usual practice for contractors to quote a price per metre run of the fence. If the price is restricted to erection only the workmanship has to be supervised. Where an all-in price, including materials, has been quoted, greater care must be taken. Since the biggest profits lie in providing cheaper materials, the specification must be detailed and checked out carefully. Look out for:

(i)   posts insufficiently driven, indicated by the cutting of tops;

(ii)   strainers not sunk deeply enough or provided with breast boards—the bottom end of the strainer may be cut off and buried when pitting it;

(iii)   the use of pressure treated posts with untreated or unsuitable strainers. The strength of the fence lies in its strainers and if treated posts are called for, strainers should be of similar specification;

(iv)   the use of reversed posts nailed through their point as stays;

(v)   all strainers making an angle to the fenceline should have at least one stay;

(vi)   the re-use of old rusty line wires from an original fence to hang new netting. This will result in early electrolysis and consequent loss of galvanising;

(vii)   the use of treated spruce instead of pine. Spruce does not take enough preservative for groundline work.

Most important of all is to ensure that the weak points are the subject of a separate specification. It is usually a mistake to ask contractors to quote on a piecework basis for extras such as watergates. These should be done on a timework basis with materials supplied by the estate.

Satisfactory Specifications

LINE WIRE FENCING. Its drawbacks have already been stated. However, in a *low ground situation* where regular inspection can be carried out on a permanent basis, an eleven wire fence of spring steel wire can be considered. At metre intervals the use of wire droppers of the type that locks onto the wires and has the ends twisted round them is strongly advocated. Wooden droppers lose staples, or only too easily get broken, and if this happens the fence is immediately suspect. Posts should not be further apart than 33 ft (10 m), with 1150 ft (350 m) intervals for strainers.

TWO-PIECE NETTING. Rylock type, hinged joint or welded mesh, to give a minimum height of 6 ft (1.83 m), strung on three line wires of spring steel and attached to it with lashing rods, make excellent deer fences. Posts in hill country should not, however, exceed 16 ft (5 m) apart, with strainers not more than 656 ft (200 m) apart. This interval can be exceeded on level terrain not subjected to snow drifting.

ONE-PIECE NETTING. The continental type strung on 3 spring steel line wires and attached by lashing rods is a good fence, the lower spacing of horizontal wires seldom allowing even hares to pass through. The spacing of posts and strainers should be as for the two-piece netting fences.

SHEEP NETTING. An alternative to welded mesh or rylock type but at the 14 gauge needed it is very much more expensive.

COMBINED FENCING. To keep out rabbits and hares—18 gauge rabbit netting backed by not less than 4 line wires should be used—with C6/90/30 rylock type on the bottom and hinged joint or welded mesh on the top.

Over the years there will no doubt be further advances in fencing practice which the deer forest manager will consider as alternatives to those mentioned in this chapter. It must be stressed, however, that many short cuts have already been tried and most found to be wanting or more expensive in the long run. The deer fence has to cope with the worst extremes of weather found in Britain. With a resourceful and determined animal trying to cross, only a well constructed and properly maintained fence is likely to fulfil its purpose.

Chapter 12   **Supplementary Feeding**

The supplementary feeding of deer in winter is carried out for three main purposes:

(i)   to lower losses through severe weather mortality;

(ii)   to improve stock leading to better heads, heavier beasts and better calving success;

(iii)   to confine deer on the ground to maintain the nucleus of a good resident stock and to discourage marauding.

The principal opposition to feeding is the usual one of cost and the problems that arise if for any reason it has to be discontinued.

Mineral blocks, hay and roots are the most common supplements but grain and 'nuts' are also extensively used. While blocks are valuable additions during winter, fodder, or a combination of feed and blocks, is of much more value especially in severe weather. If sheep are grazed close to the deer feeding area mineral blocks should be placed on posts outwith their reach.

Deer will come to the supplementary feed soon after it is put out and will disperse as soon as feeding stops. Stags are generally more easily attracted to winter feed than hinds. It is the more dominant stags that obtain most of the winter feed. In mixed groups the females are subordinate to the males. It is important, therefore, that food should be well spread out, to allow access for as many beasts as possible and to reduce the possibility of injury.

Feeding sites should be rotated to avoid over-trampling, damage to grazing or shelter belts, and to discourage the build up of disease and parasites.

Chapter 13 **Management Groups**

Although deer are not migratory animals they move over considerable distances, especially between summer and winter range. Certain estates (and hill farmers) are aware, sometimes to their cost, that while deer will winter on their ground, come spring the herds quickly disperse. However, the territory in which a herd resides is often bounded by physical features that restrain the deer from moving outwith the area. Apart, therefore, from being convenient blocks for counting purposes, those areas are ideally suited for the overall management of the local population as a single unit. While individual estates may attempt to hold permanent resident stocks, the majority of deer pay no heed to marches and it is in the best interest of all to try to manage the deer as one herd.

Joint management groups have been set up in many of the count areas; in the larger blocks it is sometimes possible and more practicable to set up more than one group if the terrain is suitable.

Ideally, all estates within an area should be members of the appropriate management group but, if the group is to be effective, membership should be extended to include all occupiers of land affected by deer in that particular area. The Forestry Commission is perhaps the most important single member in this category but agricultural interests should also be fully represented.

With the existing high density of deer and the rise in venison prices, proper management of stocks is essential with co-operation and full exchange of information between estates desirable. Efficient management of deer stocks in the area should be the prime aim of the group. It is essential to determine the optimum deer density with the minimum of acceptable pressure by deer on agricultural and forestry interests within or adjoining the management area. In this respect the loss to deer of wintering ground is an important factor. Estates cannot give up low ground to forestry or agricultural developments and expect to maintain the same numbers of deer on a reduced winter range. Management groups will be required to consider this factor and take appropriate action, by reduction of stock, provision of additional wintering facilities, by shelter belts or supplementary feeding or by acquiring low-lying land for the specific purpose of overwintering stock.

It is the Red Deer Commission's policy to encourage the formation of group management wherever possible and to give practical assistance and advice if requested.

The most important matters to be considered by groups are:

(i)   regular counts;

(ii)   an agreed policy on culling of stags and hinds;

(iii)   the provision and maintenance of good fences to avoid loss of stock through marauding on agricultural land and forests;

(iv)   a feeding programme to reduce marauding in areas where wintering ground has been encroached upon by other forms of land use;

(v)   the preservation of an overall nucleus of good stock for sporting purposes and venison production.

Financial contributions by members towards the cost of fencing and supplementary feeding to avoid out of season culling is considered of vital importance by groups already in existence, while a co-operative approach to the sale of venison has proved valuable in certain areas.

The initiative for setting up a management group must come from the estates themselves and the policy followed is largely determined by the circumstances relating to the particular area. While the Red Deer Commission will provide professional advice, they cannot give financial assistance. The Highlands and Islands Development Board, within the area for which they are responsible, are able to contribute towards the administrative costs of a management group and application should be made to the Board at Bridge House, Bank Street, Inverness.

PART IV   MISCELLANEOUS

Chapter 14   History of the Deer Problem in Scotland

It is important to appreciate the place that the wild red deer has in Scottish history, as it relates to the present legal position regarding the control and conservation of the species. Surprisingly, the red deer has been involved in events of varying significance from the mid-18th century.

What is commonly called 'the deer problem' stems from two major historical developments in the 18th and 19th centuries: namely, the social upheaval in the Highlands following the collapse of the Jacobite rising of 1745 and the Industrial Revolution.

After Culloden, the clan system was destroyed and for the first time in centuries anyone could travel safely over the whole country. Among the first to take advantage of this freedom of movement were south country sheep farmers who were quick to realise that only a very small part of the grazing potential of the northern hills was being utilised. Offering rents far in excess of anything the native tacksmen and crofters could pay—for instance, £350 was paid for the rent of a grazing in Kintail which had previously yielded only £15—they were welcomed by the landowners and before long a tide of Cheviot and Blackface sheep was spreading north. The uplands of Dunbartonshire were colonised in the 1760s and soon after the Highland Clearances began. The new stocks ranged far and wide and flocks of wedders were put out on to the high, inaccessible places which had previously been occupied only by deer. Few people were now interested in the red deer and without protection their numbers appear to have dwindled to a low ebb.

But before the conversion of the mountains into sheep runs was completed, another change was taking place. In England the Industrial Revolution was creating a new and wealthy leisured class which was already casting round for diversion. The first of the south country sportsmen were reconnoitring the Highlands only a few decades later than the sheep farmers, but the real influx did not begin until after the first quarter of the 19th century, when the trickle quickly swelled to a flood. Just as the sheep-farmers had out-bid the crofters, so the sportsman was able to out-bid the sheep-farmer, at a time when the viability of sheep farming was under some pressure. The sheep were cleared from great areas of hill and the red deer encouraged to multiply. As their numbers increased, so also did the resentment of the crofters and farmers. The dispute assumed serious proportions and came eventually to public notice.

In 1873 a Select Committee of the House of Commons was instructed 'to enquire into the laws for the protection of deer in Scotland with reference to their general bearing on the interests of the community'. This was the first of a series of enquiries, pursued at intervals over the next 50 years, which succeeded very well in depicting the problem but failed to disclose any acceptable solution. The controversy burned on, sometimes with great heat as, in 1885, when a misguided deer forest lessee, in occupation of about 200,000 acres (80,937 hectares) of shootings, sought to have a cottar interdicted from grazing a pet lamb on one of his deer forests and in 1887 when the Lewis crofters marched from one end of the island to the other driving the deer before them into the sea. But more often the problem took the form of parochial feuding and bickering.

The first effective deer control measure reached the Statute Book in 1948 when the Agriculture (Scotland) Act gave the occupiers of agricultural holdings and enclosed woodlands, or a nominee, an inalienable right to kill any deer found on their enclosed land and to dispose of the carcases. This right is unaffected by close seasons, but only the occupier in person can shoot at night. The Act also empowered the Secretary of State, in certain circumstances, to authorise the killing of deer on any land, but it was soon apparent that this authority was so complicated as to be virtually unusable.

Around 1950 attention was focused on deer poaching. Meat rationing and limited police powers had resulted in wide-spread commercial-scale poaching attended by much cruelty. This activity might have been dealt with by straightforward anti-poaching legislation but poachers were not alone in taking advantage of the high price of venison. A number of people with a perfectly legitimate right to kill deer were also prepared to supply this market at all seasons, regardless of the condition of the deer. Since measures aimed at curbing poaching would have left this trade unhampered, the conservationists urged the introduction of close seasons. This was opposed by agriculturists and foresters on the grounds that the provisions of the 1948 Agriculture (Scotland) Act, intended for their protection against deer, were largely unworkable, that the numbers and range of the red deer were increasing in many districts, causing anxiety and loss to those who had to earn a livelihood from the land, and that further protection for the deer could only make matters worse. Close seasons, they argued, should not be introduced until deer numbers were brought under control.

Faced with this impasse the Secretary of State, in 1952, appointed a Committee under the chairmanship of Sheriff Maconochie 'to consider the desirability of introducing a close season or seasons for deer in Scotland.' The inquiry lasted two years but failed to reach agreement, the majority being in favour of the introduction of close seasons with appropriate safeguards for agricultural interests, the minority—the three farming members—recommending that close seasons should not be introduced until deer numbers had been reduced to a satisfactory level and marauding deer exterminated.

Despite these apparently irreconcilable differences, both interests were anxious to reach agreement and discussions were begun under the auspices of the Nature Conservancy. In 1956 a compromise was reached and a joint approach made to the Secretary of State recommending appropriate legislation. Two years later a Bill was introduced into the House of Lords. It ultimately emerged in 1959 as the Deer (Scotland) Act which, among other things, required the Secretary of State to constitute a Red Deer Commission to have the general functions of furthering the conservation and control of red deer. The Act also made provision for the introduction of close seasons on 21 October 1962.

By 1977 the deer population in Scotland had risen to 270,000 and pressure on forestry and agriculture had not abated. Competition from other land users on the essential deer wintering grounds resulted in a loss of shelter and food supply in the traditional deer forests and consequently put pressure on the deer to find alternative facilities.

By 1979 the land on which deer could be found amounted to 7·75 million acres (3·14 million hectares). Following two severe winters, numbers had reduced to 255,000 with, perhaps more significantly, a substantial reduction in calf survival.

For the future deer managers will have to consider the effect of an extending deer range with the consequent pressures on farm and forest, intensified by a continuing reduction in the availability of wintering ground. The optimum deer population will be determined not by the presence of vast tracts of high summer range but by the ground on which the deer can survive during winter without adversely affecting other land users.

Chapter 15   The Red Deer Commission

In 1959 Parliament gave the Red Deer Commission the responsibility for the general functions of furthering the conservation and control of red deer.

Members are appointed by the Secretary of State for Scotland and the Commission consists of a Chairman, one nominee of the Nature Conservancy Council, one nominee of the Natural Environment Research Council, five members representing landowning and sporting interests and five representing farmers and crofters. Its headquarters are at Knowsley, 82 Fairfield Road, Inverness; telephone number Inverness (0463) 31751.

The Commission deal with a wide variety of matters including the broad problems of land use, deer management, the effects of forestry planting programmes, deer farming, legislation and scientific research on red deer in Scotland. Red deer census work is leading increasingly to the formation of co-operative management schemes between neighbouring estates and the continuing pressure of other land uses emphasises the problem of future management. Deer control in the face of competitive land usage still carries a high priority.

The work is controlled by the Commission's Secretary assisted by a small administrative staff, while a well-equipped field staff is responsible for the practical work of conducting the census, calf marking, assisting estates with their annual culls, undertaking management studies and investigating and dealing with complaints of marauding deer.

The Commission have a statutory duty with extensive powers to prevent damage to agriculture and forestry by red deer. Skilled stalkers with transport and equipment are available to investigate complaints (usually within 48 hours) and to take direct action where necessary anywhere in Scotland. The opportunity to take the appropriate steps against marauding deer is, however, always given to the persons with the right to shoot the deer in question and it is only when they are unable or unwilling to do so that the Commission's stalkers are authorised to shoot. Persons with a deer damage problem which they are not legally entitled to resolve themselves (see Chapter 16), should in the first instance attempt to seek a solution locally by contacting whoever has the right to shoot the deer. If satisfactory action cannot be obtained they should report the matter to the Red Deer Commission as soon as possible.

Enforcement of the law regarding poaching, close seasons and shooting at night are for the Police and do not come within the Commission's remit. *Policy and associated legislation with regard to these matters are a vital part of the Commission's function.*

From time to time the Commission publish advisory material both for deer managers and those faced with damage caused by red deer; most of these pamphlets are obtainable from the Commission without charge. The Commission also submit an annual report on its work to the Secretary of State for Scotland.

Chapter 16   Deer and the Law

The following paragraphs set out a few aspects of the law in Scotland which might be of value to stalkers and deer managers. *It is emphasised, however, that this chapter has no standing as a legal document.*

The Right to Kill

Deer are wild animals and living in their natural state belong to no one. The right to kill them goes primarily with the ownership of the land they are on and to a much more limited extent with the occupancy. Excluding the specific circumstances mentioned below, deer may not be killed in the close seasons or during the hours of darkness, ie between the end of the first hour after sunset and the beginning of the last hour before sunrise.

What Right has the Occupier to Kill Deer?

The occupier of an agricultural holding or of enclosed woodlands has the right to kill deer found on his enclosed land and to take possession of the carcases at any time regardless of close seasons and to authorise anybody else to do so **except at night**. Only the occupier is permitted to shoot at night.

The tenant of an agricultural holding has no right to shoot red deer outwith the enclosed part of his holding unless he has written permission from his landlord and then he may only do so in the appropriate open seasons unless otherwise authorised in writing by the Red Deer Commission.

If any tenant cannot deal with marauding deer on his land he should invite his landlord to do so but, failing action on the part of the landlord, he should consult the Red Deer Commission.

Catching of Live Deer

Deer can be captured alive in season by a person with the legal right to take or kill them, or by someone authorised in writing by that person, in a manner *which does not cause unecessary suffering to the animal*. With the increasing demand from deer farmers for stock, substantial prices are being obtained, especially for breeding hinds, and capture of live deer can be a profitable operation. Hinds taken in this manner can be considered as part of the appropriate cull. Capturing deer in numbers is a fairly recent innovation and various methods are at present being examined.

Until now darting of deer at feeding sites has been effective. Owners considering taking deer alive are advised to examine carefully, with expert advice if necessary, all possible methods available.

Darting

The use of darting equipment and the appropriate drugs is a matter for the expert and should not be attempted without the assistance of a fully qualified and legally certificated operator. Weapons and ammunition are closely controlled and fall within the terms of the Firearms Act 1968 and a firearms certificate is required where necessary. In addition, the authority of the Secretary of State for Scotland and the police is required for the possession of weapons and ammunition.

So far as drugs are concerned, the terms of the Misuse of Drugs Act 1971 makes it obligatory for any operator to obtain a licence from the Home Office. Moreover, strict conditions have to be fulfilled.

Unless used sensibly, immobilising drugs can be dangerous not only to the animal but also to the operator. Expert advice should always be obtained before any darting operation is undertaken.

Compensation for Damage by Deer

Compensation may be claimed by a tenant from his landlord for damage caused by deer under the terms of Section 15 of the Agricultural Holdings (Scotland) Act 1949 and Section 19 of the Deer (Scotland) Act 1959.

Close Seasons

The close seasons are:

for red deer	Stags—21 October to 30 June annually.
	Hinds—16 February to 20 October annually.
for fallow deer	Male—1 May to 31 July both dates inclusive.
	Female—16 February to 20 October both dates inclusive.
for roe deer	Male—21 October to 30 April both dates inclusive.
	Female—1 March to 20 October both dates inclusive.
for sika deer	Male—1 May to 31 July both dates inclusive.
	Female—16 February to 20 October both dates inclusive.

Firearms

Deer may only be killed by shooting with a firearm as defined in the Firearms Act

1968, other than an automatic weapon or a weapon discharging a noxious liquid. There is no other restriction on type or calibre.

General

The main legislation covering deer is the Deer (Scotland) Act 1959 and the Deer (Amendment) (Scotland) Act 1967 which give the Red Deer Commission certain powers relating to the conservation and control of deer. The Act sets out offences such as poaching and unlawful possession of deer and firearms which are, of course, police matters. It also empowers the Commission to give advice to estate owners or anybody interested in or affected by deer and to collaborate with other bodies in research into matters of scientific or practical importance relating to deer.

The rights of an occupier of an agricultural holding or woodland are laid down in Section 43(1) of the Agriculture (Scotland) Act 1948 and should be read with the Agricultural Holdings (Scotland) Act 1949.

There is also legislation, namely the Sale of Venison (Scotland) Act 1968, to cover the examination by the Red Deer Commission of venison dealers' records with a view to ascertaining the total number of deer purchased by them from estates and other sources.

Appendix

Appendix A   Teeth and Age in Scottish Red Deer A Practical Guide to Age Assessment

Being able to estimate the ages of deer—both live and dead—is of importance and interest to those involved in deer management and research. Good stock husbandry depends upon it, as does research on the performance (growth, development, breeding success and longevity) of wild deer. Classifying the animals simply as 'young', 'prime', or 'old', may be sufficient for some purposes, but for others it may be necessary to place the deer as accurately as possible into their year classes. Estimating age with live deer is especially difficult, and it depends very much on individual experience. But much can be learned by examining the teeth and other features of newly shot deer, and many stalkers are well aware of this. However, unless stalkers have opportunities to examine deer of known age (eg ones marked as calves and shot as adults) they can gain little understanding of the relationship between the dental and other characteristics of the deer and their actual ages in years.

The first serious research on the accurate assessment of age with red deer was done by German biologists around 50 years ago. By the early 1930's they had described the rates of tooth eruption and wear, and developed another method based on growth layers in the dentine (=ivory) of incisor teeth (Müller-Using, 1932; Eidmann, 1933). These annual layers in dentine are similar to the growth increments in trees, but to expose and interpret them effectively requires much practice and skill.

Other work began during the late 1950's to test the applicability of various methods of age estimation to Scottish red deer, using material from deer of known age (Mitchell, 1963, 1967; Lowe, 1967)—a by-product of the tagging of calves to study their movements. One outcome was the development of a method based on growth layers in dental cement which grows around the roots of all teeth, but also forms a thick pad below the crowns on molar teeth; see Figure 1. Although these layers are a little easier to expose and interpret than those in the dentine, the method is not convenient for routine management purposes. The main values of this technique are in research, for example, in checking other methods of age estimation, as outlined below.

Material collected by the R.D.C. and I.T.E. includes jaws from over one hundred deer of known age (from deer tagged in several study areas), and much larger numbers of jaws (from a wider range of localities) which have been aged by the cement layer method. Arranging these jaws by sex, age, and place of origin,

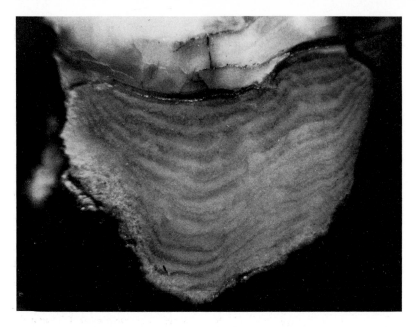

Figure 1 Magnified section of the cement pad on a lower first molar tooth. The number of broad white layers gives the age of the deer in years—in this example 13 layers. The tooth was from a hind which died in March, so the age would be 13 years and 9 months.

for visual comparisons on the rates of tooth eruption and wear, gave several interesting results.

In brief, we found no obvious differences in dental appearance between stags and hinds in each age class, and no consistent differences between deer of the same age from different populations. The patterns and rates of replacement of milk incisors and premolars were remarkably constant. Although there was considerable variation in the rate of wear on incisor teeth, both individually and between populations, there was much less variation in the wear rates on premolars and molars. It is not clear why such differences exist between the incisors and the cheek teeth, but, because of their more consistent rate of wear, the cheek teeth provide the best guide to age in mature deer. It is worth adding here that the dental features typifying each class of Scottish deer appear remarkably similar to those illustrated for German red deer (Müller-Using, 1971). Therefore, it may be that most, if not all, red deer populations show much the same rates of tooth eruption and wear—a somewhat surprising but potentially useful finding.

Before describing the dental features in relation to age, some general comments on the naming of teeth may be helpful. Biologists usually express the tooth arrangement in a mammal as a 'dental formula'. Small letters are used for milk teeth and

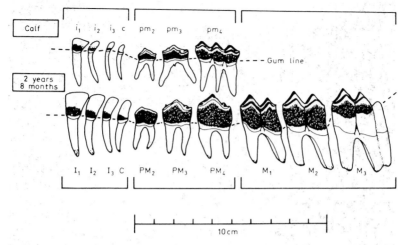

Figure 2 Milk teeth from a young calf (2 months) and permanent teeth from a late 2-year-old. Note that the fourth incisiform tooth is really a modified canine, and that the premolars are numbered '2', '3', and '4'. Although the milk teeth and permanent teeth differ mostly in size, the last milk premolar (pm 4) and the last permanent premolar (PM 4) differ considerably in structure. The development of the last molar (M 3) is an important feature in 2-year-olds, ie the last cusp is either just cutting through the jaw or has just done so.

capitals for permanent teeth, with 'I' for incisors, 'C' for canines (='tusks'), 'PM' for premolars, and 'M' for molars. The numbers of upper and lower teeth (one side only) are shown in the form of fractions. Thus, a young calf and an adult deer would be expressed as follows.

Young calf: $i\dfrac{0}{3}\ c\dfrac{I}{I}\ pm\dfrac{3}{3}$ (and $M\dfrac{I}{I}$ after a few months)

Adult deer: $I\dfrac{0}{3}\ C\dfrac{I}{I}\ PM\dfrac{3}{3}\ M\dfrac{3}{3}$

Ignoring the upper teeth for present purposes, these formulae simply show that a young red deer calf has seven milk teeth on each jaw bone, with an extra tooth (the first molar) developing during the first 3–4 months of life. An adult red deer has a total of ten permanent teeth on each jaw. There are two other minor points which should be mentioned, if only for scientific accuracy. In deer, the lower canine tooth looks like an incisor, and is often mistakenly called the fourth incisor. Here, for convenience, we refer to these four cutting teeth as 'incisiform teeth'. Finally, the most primitive mammals have four premolar teeth, and the deer have lost the first, leaving the second third and fourth. Figure 2 shows the appearance of the milk teeth and permanent teeth in red deer, and their correct name-symbols.

The presence of gum tissues (fresh or dried) on a jaw can make age assessment difficult, especially in the case of a mature or old individual. So it is best to clean jaws first, either by boiling them for an hour or two, or by allowing them to rot down for several months in damp conditions, ie in deep grass or in plastic bags. Although incisor teeth tend to fall out from cleaned jaws, they are of less value than cheek teeth in age assessment. Teeth in cleaned jaws tend to split and fragment if they are stored for long periods in warm dry conditions; cool damp conditions, or painting jaws with clear varnish, can prevent disintegration.

The main illustrations given here (Figures 4–6) show typical rows of cheek teeth from red deer killed in late autumn, some of the older ages being omitted for simplicity. Most are from wild deer of known age (ie selected jaws from our collections), but some of the older ones were assessed from their cement layers. The oldest one is from a park stag of known age ($19\frac{1}{2}$ years), since wild deer over 17 years old are quite rare. There is a much larger margin of error in assessing age from tooth wear in older deer; variability in rate and pattern of wear increases with age.

Calves, yearlings, and 2-year-old deer are identified from their patterns of milk ('calf') teeth and permanent teeth. As shown in Figure 2, milk incisor teeth are much smaller than permanent incisors. Likewise, milk premolars are smaller than permanent ones, but 'pm 4' has a triple crown and root arrangement which is diagnostic. The main dental characteristics of the first three age classes are summarised in the table opposite: see also Figure 3.

With jaws collected during the normal shooting seasons, there are rarely any difficulties in separating the first three age classes. Indeed, calves and yearlings may be identified simply from their incisor teeth: if the incisors are all milk then the animal is a calf, and if they are mixed then the animal is a yearling. Both of these classes have milk premolars also, but calves show only one molar and yearlings two. Intermediate stages of tooth replacement occur amongst the three year classes, of course, when animals are examined outside the normal shooting seasons, but these are easy enough to interpret with experience and practice. Premature tooth replacement is very much rarer than delayed replacement; indeed we have not seen any cases of exceptionally early replacement which overlapped the age class above. The main kinds of delayed replacement are as follows. Some stunted yearlings retain their milk incisiform teeth, although clearly showing two molar teeth. Backward 2-year-olds may still retain their milk premolars, or even one milk incisor, whilst having the three molars normally present at that age. So even these cases are not too difficult to classify, given the rule that delayed development of some teeth is more common than premature development.

From 3 years, each age class is characterised by the relative amount of wear on the premolar and molar crowns. A useful distinction between 2- and 3-year-olds is the last cusp of the third molar (the last tooth) which is unstained and unworn in the former, but slightly stained and blunted in the latter. A further method of

	Calf (6 months)	Yearling ($1\frac{1}{2}$ years)	$2\frac{1}{2}$-years-old
'Incisors'	4 milk	1–2 permanent, others milk	4 permanent
Premolars	3 milk	3 milk	3 permanent— loose, widely spaced, with hollow fragile roots.
Molars	1 permanent— with hollow fragile roots.	2 permanent— first with constricted roots, second with hollow fragile roots.	3 permanent— unworn, third molar with hollow fragile roots and last cusp just cutting the jaw bone.
Total number of teeth per jaw	8	9	10

separating these two age classes is to pull out the last premolar tooth and examine its roots. Widely-open fragile roots indicate a 2-year-old, whereas thicker almost-closed roots show the animal to be a 3-year-old.

In comparing jaws with our illustrations, it will be seen that patterns of wear are variable. All the teeth are worn evenly in some deer, whilst others show most wear in the middle of the tooth row. This has to be taken into account; ages are assessed from the overall amount of wear. Our own tests on this method indicate that ages can be determined with almost absolute accuracy in the first three or four year classes. Up to around ten years, ages can be assessed to the nearest year on average, but with progressively increasing error thereafter.

We were asked to prepare this new guide, as copies of our earlier one (published in the R.D.C. Report for 1968) have now run out. In doing so, we have been able to make use of the larger collections of known-age jaws which have built up over the last ten years. Curiously enough, even with the new material, we have found little to criticise about the standard jaws shown in the earlier guide; they were remarkably similar to the ones given here. Nonetheless, we are very grateful

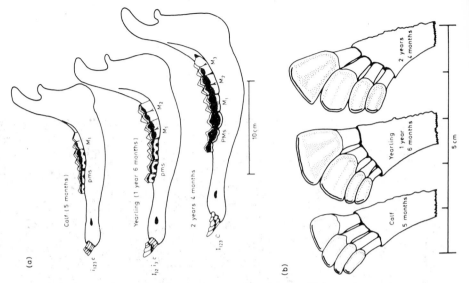

Figure 3 The main feature of calves, yearlings, and 2-year-olds. The upper diagrams show the appearance of the complete jaws, and the lower ones show the incisor teeth from each. Note that a yearling may show one, two, or even three permanent incisiform teeth.

Figures 4, 5 and 6 The cheek teeth from deer of various ages, ranging from a calf to a 19½-year-old. Most are from animals of known age, but some of the older ones (labelled 'est.') have been assessed from tooth layers.

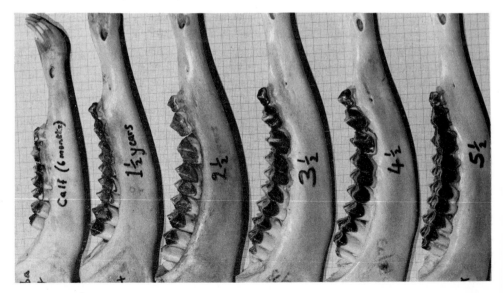

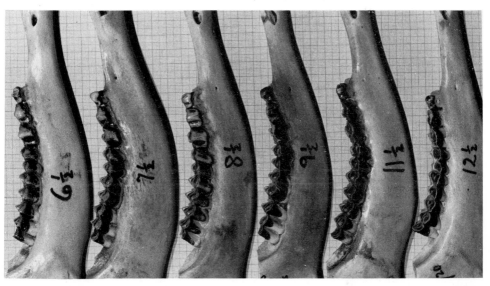

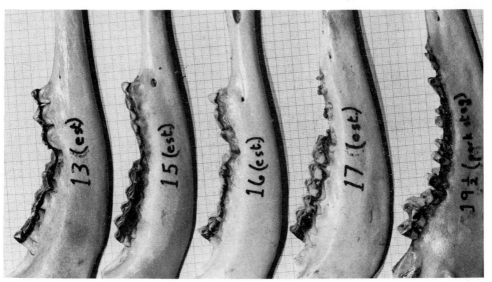

indeed to the many stalkers who have kindly sent in the jaws, ear-tags, and other details of any tagged deer they have shot or found dead. May they continue to do so, as the material and information is required for other purposes besides making up collections of known age jaws. Finally, we thank the editors of the Journal of Animal Ecology for permission to republish Figures 2 and 3.

Brian Mitchell
Institute of Terrestrial Ecology
BANCHORY

Richard W. Youngson
The Red Deer Commission
INVERNESS

References

Eidmann, H. M. (1933). Alterserscheinung am Gebiss des Rothirsches als Grundlage zur exakten Bestimung des Lebensalters.
Schaper, Hannover.

Lowe, V. P. W. (1967). Teeth as indicators of age with special reference to Red deer (*Cervus elaphus*) of known age from Rhum.
J. Zool., Lond. 152, 137–153.

Mitchell, B. (1963). Determination of age in Scottish red deer from growth layers in dental cement.
Nature, Lond. 198, 350–351.

Mitchell, B. (1967). Growth layers in dental cement for determining the age of red deer (*Cervus elaphus* L.).
J. Anim. Ecol. 36, 279–293.

Müller-Using, D. (1932). Rotwildalter-Merkblatt der Gesellschaft für Jagdkunde.
Merkblatt 35.

Müller-Using, D. (1971, 5 Auflage). Rotwildalter-Merkblatt.
Deutschen Jagdschutz-Verbandes.

Printed in Scotland by Her Majesty's Stationery Office at HMSO Press, Edinburgh
Dd 0630404 K13 1/81 (17533)